PARISH, PRIEST & PEOPLE

New Leadership for the Local Church

PARISH, PRIEST & PEOPLE

New Leadership for the Local Church

by

Andrew Greeley, Mary Durkin, John Shea
David Tracy and William McCready

THE THOMAS MORE PRESS
Chicago, Illinois

ISBN 0-88347-131-0

Table of Contents

Introduction

The question of scale might be put another way: what is needed in all these matters is to discriminate, to get things sorted out. For every activity there is a certain appropriate scale, and the more active and intimate the activity, the smaller the number of people that can take part, the greater is the number of such relationship arrangements that need to be established.

from *Small is Beautiful*
by E. F. Schumacher

A STUDY of pastoral leadership in the local church is, to a very great extent, a study of the scale of religious life. There are undoubtedly global issues which are important to the study of religious beliefs and behaviors, but religious experiences exist within individuals and their social networks and these are found at the primary levels of society—in families, neighborhoods and local communities across the nation.

This book is the result of an interdisciplinary collaboration between social scientists and theologians who attempted to join their perspectives into a coherent view of the phenomenon of the local church. Discussions, meetings, lunches and exchanges of drafts were techniques used liberally by the authors and the result was a true cross-fertilization of ideas and perspectives.

Several principles guided our efforts and it may well assist the reader in understanding our multi-disciplinary perspective if these are clarified at the outset. The theologians all expressed a preference for beginning with detailed human experiences and using them as a basis for theological reflection. As they perceive their role, it is not simply to evaluate and elucidate the words of other theological writers, although there are appropriate references and footnotes in this text. Rather, they include human experiences and stories as material to which they can apply their skills of theological reflection and interpretation. The theory behind this process as well as examples of the process itself are delineated in this report. Of particular interest to those responsible for training people for various ministerial roles are the materials in chapters 13 and 14 which apply this model of reflecting-upon-experience to the task of ministerial education.

The sociologists also espouse a perspective which begins with experience in the form of social research data and moves toward modeling and interpreting the stories contained within these data. The techniques of social science research allow us to listen to the lives of people in systematic and disciplined ways so that our descriptions and inferences reflect the actual behaviors and attitudes of people and not just what the researcher wants to believe.

Both the theologians and sociologists bring to this project intimate personal experiences of local church, as well as their professional skills and resources. It is difficult to live in Chicago and not be immersed in the local—the neighborhood, the parish and the community. It is at one and the same time a resource and a potential obstacle to the observer to inhabit such an environment. On the one hand we have sensitivities to the scale of life and to the social and religious structures which enable humans to successfully cope with their mass-urban environment in ways that inhibit loss of personalism and human contact. On the other hand we are subject to the criticism that Chicago is unrepresentative of the rest of the country and that the urban experience of neighborhood and parish is no longer applicable to the more transient populations of the rest of the country. This might be true if we felt that such populations had nothing in common with their urbanized relatives, but such is not the case.

Similar criticism is possible given that we have focused on the Catholic experience of local church rather than on a broad interdenominational survey. Even if such a broad-based approach were possible within the scope of this project, and it can be clearly argued that it was not, it was not the way to begin this investigation of a new and challenging area of the relationship between theology and sociology and how they might be brought to bear jointly on salient issues of concern to those responsible for the well-being of the local church, whatever its identity.

The most unequivocal response to those potential complaints is that this project is an exercise in the study of "what works," as opposed to the kind of research which concentrates on social pathologies as the source for data. We have elected to start our investigations within that area which we know best since this is a preliminary effort which we hope others will emulate and pursue. The traditional Catholic parish as found in the neighborhoods of Chicago and its surrounding suburbs has elements which highlight the interaction between theological foundations and social structures. The examination of ways in which local church happens and the factors which enable it to develop productively needs to begin in a setting conducive to allowing the observers to use all their powers, whether they are derived from scholarly disciplines or from the common human experiences of living within supportive communities, institutions and social structures. Once these requirements are voiced, the choice of a research context is easier. One begins where one has been all along. You begin by looking at your home, your neighborhood and by reflecting on your own experiences and those of the people you know best. There will be time for comparative studies later; the initial foraging into the unknown is best started from that which we know well. Our first questions have to do with that which we do not know about our immediate surroundings and our first reflections have to do with looking at what we have always experienced, but in a brand new way.

The first part of our report consists of reflections upon various aspects of the local religious community or the local church. In the first chapter we present descriptions of two parishes and offer reflections upon the similarities and differences between them. These stories point out that parishes are places where people take root and where their religious sensibilities begin to take concrete forms. The second chapter is more sociological and here we focus on the facts and data which reveal the fallacies contained within the conventional wisdom which concludes that secularization has made religion insignificant and that modern men do not build intimate communities. Religious development in the local context is explored within chapter three and the concept of "sacred space" is discussed as a powerful factor in enabling people's religious perspectives to grow from insight into action. Chapters four and five bring the perspectives of systematic and pastoral theology to bear on the experiences of the local church. Insights derived from experiences are combined with approaches to people which stress listening and reflection to produce a theological vision of parish into which we can insert our questions and discussions about the role of parish leadership. These chapters, especially the fifth, set the context for the following section.

The second part examines leadership in the local church from a variety of perspectives utilizing the insights and conclusions of the first part. Leadership is defined with strokes both broad and narrow, but throughout most of this section we discuss priestly leadership at the local parish level, since that is the aspect of religious authority with which most people come into contact. Chapter five begins with some stories of authority and follows the previous pattern of stating experiences first and then following up with reflection and interpretation. Religious authority is subject to the same principles which govern other uses of authority and a salient point in this chapter is that "leading" is less related to giving orders than to telling stories and engaging in "disconcerting behavior." Religious leadership is an exercise in being clever about revealing the graciousness of reality, not in ruling over people's behavior and feelings.

In chapter seven we apply the sociological principles of community and the sacred to our study of parish leadership. Rather than deny the power contained in the leadership role of priest, we have explored the ways in which this power becomes manifest in the life of the parish. The power contained in the symbol of religious celebrant is examined, interpreted and reflected back upon our description of parish structure, revealing that priests are powerful, critical, leaders in the parish—even if they fail to recognize it some of the time.

In the eighth chapter the concept of "Christ and culture" is used to develop reflections on the theological basis for local religious leadership as revealed in the experiences of parochial life and the writings of theologians. In chapter nine we examine the relationship between the role of the priest and the religious socialization of the people in the parish. This discussion includes insights derived from "natural ministries" and concludes with some speculative thoughts about the reverse socialization process—the impact of people upon their religious leaders.

The next three chapters are about a specific aspect of religious leadership at the local level and in them we examine the role of the priest, the relationship between leadership and social justice and professionalism in leadership. In the tenth chapter we explore the role of the priest, especially as a "connector" between the articulation of the religious vision and the concrete life of the local community. In chapter eleven we describe the role of the religious leader in presenting the social commitment of the church and then motivating the lay people to honor that commitment. The concept of "manifestation" is used here to explore the role of the leader in presenting the theologically based vision as immersed in the varieties of social reality which populate our experiences. In chapter twelve we discuss the need for professional skills and demeanor and identity for the religious leader. These leadership skills are not those of the authoritarian ruler, rather they are those possessed by consensual and coalition building leaders. Skills of articulation rather than coercion are stressed for religious leaders who hope to have any followers.

The third part consists of two chapters which go into finer detail about the education of the religious leader and the development of "religious imagination." In chapter thirteen we focus on the skills of articulation that appropriately belong to the religious leader. Preaching is paramount and the data indicate that this is an extremely important aspect of leadership as far as the laity are concerned. There are many ways religious leaders articulate their vision and "obtain consent" from church members for that vision, and these are explored and discussed in the context of ministerial training as well as practice. In chapter fourteen the concept of "religious imagination" is introduced as a critical factor in the development of religious leaders. This characteristic, which is closely related to the creative imagination, enables the religious leader to link experiences together so that those listening will always be able to see something new in what is being said. This is a quality of the storyteller, the poet and quite appropriately of the priest. The images and symbols which inhabit the persona of the faithful need to be touched and reflected back to them by their religious leaders. This is the task of the religious imagination and it is a skill that can be taught.

The final part contains one chapter and that is where we speculate and suggest directions for the future as well as recommendations for the present. The materials developed during the body of the book are assembled and lessons drawn. The preliminary nature of this effort notwithstanding, this final chapter offers insights and suggestions which could keep those concerned with the development of religious leadership busy and hopefully started off in new directions for the foreseeable future.

Since the writing of this volume was a genuine interdisciplinary activity it is difficult to say who contributed what to which section. The following is a listing of where the individual author's contributions generally wound up:

Mary G. Durkin: Chapters 1, 5, 6, 13 and the overall editing, compiling and rewriting

Andrew M. Greeley: Chapters 2, 3, 6, 7, 11, 13, 14, and 15

William C. McCready: Chapters 2, 3, 9, 11 and 12
John Shea: Chapters 3, 5, 10 and 12
David Tracy: Chapters 4, 8, and 11
Typing, transcription and other editorial and secretarial tasks were performed by Mss. Alice Burns, Georgianna Duffy and Mary Kotecki.

Perhaps the most striking characteristic of this project is not the interdisciplinary nature of the work, nor the specific focus of the heritage and communities we selected to investigate, but rather the return to the scale of religious life as a principal criterion by which we examine how well we are doing. That question, "How am I doing?" is a basic religious question in the lives of people and it has its greatest meaning at the local level. It is currently fashionable to declare that one is opposed to particularism and all its attendant problems, but the particular is where we all begin. Obviously we do not have to end up there, but to deny the particularistic nature of our origins is to shut ourselves off from the richest and most productive material for our religious reflection and growth that we possess.

Our concentration on the various aspects of the local religious community constantly reminds us that there are appropriate proportions for certain human activities. Loyalty, trust, intimacy and experiencing the graciousness of reality begin to happen only in the most supportive and intimate of settings. The family and neighborhood provide the basis for these sensibilities and the religious leadership experienced at these levels determines much of what we are able to perceive as our religious horizons expand.

The image of pastoral leadership which is examined and developed in this book is not the guidance counselor but rather the "happy, hopeful person who smiles." The authors are fond of using stories to begin their reflections in the various sections of this book. Perhaps it is appropriate to end this introduction with a story about this sort of pastoral leadership and ministry as it was experienced by an acquaintance during a very difficult period of living.

A woman, no longer exactly young but not very old either, was left the task of taking her elderly, senile mother to a nursing home while her siblings were out of town on vacation. She visited the place they had selected and was quite disturbed by what she felt was a lack of empathy on the part of the person in the admission's office to whom she had turned for some advice on just how to proceed. It wasn't that this administrator was uncaring or incompetent, but there was a lack of sparkle and life and understanding which the woman felt was very necessary if her mother was to be well cared for in this setting.

A friend recommended another facility and she decided to go and see what the place was like. The chief administrator met her and introduced her to an associate who took her around the building. (The reason he could not do it himself was that he had just put on his wading boots to help out with an emergency repair of a frozen pipe, he said, smiling.) When she greeted the various elderly residents she met on her tour, most returned her greeting with a smile and a pleasant word. The guide was not above joking with her and showing that she understood a great deal about what she and her mother and her family were going through. This institution had not lost its sense of humor about itself and therefore was able to elicit humor and hope from those who lived and worked there.

When the young woman went back to the first home she asked to see the pastoral minister, a Catholic sister who worked three days a week at the home. She related these various experiences and conversations and impressions to this sister and asked for some advice. Rather than getting

15

the "well-what-do-you-think-you-should-do" kind of counseling response, this sister helped the woman reflect on her experiences and see that she had indeed been looking for some specific characteristics in the people and place that would be caring for her mother. The happy, hopeful, smiling demeanor of the second institution was attractive because it touched chords of the woman's own religious perspective and heritage. The pastoral minister noted that both places were competent and well-administered, but she helped the woman come to a confident understanding of what her own criteria, based on her own life experiences with her mother, actually were. She began with the experiences and built her pastoral approach from that point. She made it possible for the woman to believe in "hopeful and smiling" institutions; in this way the minister elicited the basic response to the graciousness of reality which was at the core of the woman's own religious perspective.

The vision of pastoral leadership at the local level which is presented in this book is a blend of the ancient storyteller, the urban precinct captain, the mad Irish poet, the religious prophet and the caring, smiling family friend. This vision comes from our experiences, both personal and professional, and it is intended to suggest one way in which religious leadership can be structured. There may be other ways, but this one is at least based on experiences which have worked and which contained the insights of what can work in the future. New challenges face religious leadership because the faithful communities are being placed in new social contexts. We hope that the subsequent chapters will be helpful to those who are interested in meeting these challenges.

PART ONE

The Local Religious Community

CHAPTER 1

Stories from Two Parishes

IN the interest of adhering to the dictum to be up-front about where we stand, we begin this study of pastoral leadership in the local church admitting that we have a positive bias toward the possibilities of a local church. Our bias grows out of personal experience, sociological analysis and theological reflection. We begin with some reflections on personal experience of parish because that is where it all began for us. Contrary to much of the literature on the Catholic immigrant experience and its neighborhood parish that is written by alienates, most people of the immigrant era had far more positive than negative feeling about their local community. We are among their descendents who have positive feelings about the parishes of our youth. Even now, when many local parishes are floundering due to inept leadership, some of us belong to local parishes that are also thriving religious communities.

We will consider the experience of one of the authors, who grew up in a parish that "worked" and now lives in another parish with the same distinction. The story of these two parishes exemplifies why we feel, based on our experiences, that local neighborhood/parish is an important basis for religious community. We realize that in many instances this basis is not sufficiently utilized, but we see many possibilities for religious growth in geographical parishes. We sense that our positive experience of parish gives hints of the potential within most parishes.

Our story of these two parishes—St. Angela, a West Side Chicago parish during the 40's and 50's and Mary, Seat of Wisdom, a suburban Chicago parish in the 70's—has its prologue in the immigrant urban parishes of Chicago during the massive movement of people from Europe to the United States. We suspect that similar experiences of immigrant parishes would be found in other large urban centers of the same period. In Chicago, our grandparents settled in Holy Family, St. Charles Borromeo, Our Lady of Sorrows if they were West Side Irish, or Our Lady of Pompeii if they were Italian, or Holy Trinity or St. Stanislaus Kostka if they were Polish, or some other parish that allowed them to put down their "roots" in a place with others like themselves.

These neighborhood parishes were a product of the Catholic immigrant experience—the west of Ireland or a southern Polish or Italian village set down in the middle of a New World metropolis, protecting the faith, the ethnic identity and the human dignity of the immigrants during the traumas of adjustment to American life. Maybe the city laborer was simply a "shanty Irishman" to those for whom he toiled; but when he returned to his neighborhood/parish, he found a sense of belonging, a sense of shared identity with his neighbors. While such communities were certainly defensive and narrow, they also generated extraordinary warmth and loyalty among most of their members. Religiously, there was a common faith structure that saw salvation of the individual soul through obedience to the laws of God and the Church and through participation in the sacramental system.

St. Angela, during the forties and fifties, was one generation removed from the immigrant parishes of the poor ghetto areas. It also was one step removed from the poverty of the depression. Life for the child was one of relative comfort and one of complacency about identity. If the adults of the community felt any doubts about their place in the American society, they did not share these misgivings with their children. Their embrace of the war effort was an example of how they demonstrated their loyalty to America. Community organizations, such as block clubs and zone groups, gave Catholics the opportunity to interact with other community members in a patriotic endeavor. This cooperation reinforced their belief that they were "good" Americans.

The younger generation never questioned or considered that others might question their loyalty. They were secure about Catholics belonging in American society. Evidence of this can be found in the practice, common in most Chicago parishes of that time (and even today in some parishes) of identifying one's "place" as the parish. When you left the boundaries of St. Angela, whether you were a young person or an adult, you proudly informed anyone wanting to know where you lived that you were from St. Angela. Only if you encountered a non-Catholic would you mention Austin, the designated name for that area of the city. Since most of the peers of the blue-collar workers of the parish were also Catholic, this identifying mark immediately "placed" the person using it. Even the few business and professional men within the community usually belonged to the Knights of Columbus which allowed them to use the parish as an identification. The overwhelming majority of young people attended Catholic high school where there was stiff competition between parish groups.

For the people of St. Angela belonging to the parish continued to give them a sense of identity. It could be summed up as a pervasive, though unspoken, feeling that "We belong to the parish and belonging is good."

The common faith structure that united the immigrants and gave them a strong sense of belonging also united the children and grandchildren who lived in St. Angela. In the midst of the ambiguities of life, emphasized by the war and tied up with the inevitable stress of family life, the neighborhood/parish projected an image of an ordered reality. There was a feeling that here there was "a place for everything and everything in its place." Since the official representatives of the message of ordered reality, the priests and nuns, were, for the most part, benign, they projected an interpretation of the Ordered Reality as benign.

There were, it seems in retrospect, three levels of religious thought operative in St. Angela. First, there was the basic dogma of the Catholic tradition which, when correctly interpreted, offered a positive world-view. Then there was the official and quasi-official interpretation of the dogma that often ignored this positive world-view and emphasized law, sin, impurity, etc. And finally there was the personal and/or familial interpretation of God that was developed out of the experience of religious questions in people's lives.

An example of these levels of interpretation could be seen in the doctrine of creation and incarnation which should lead to a positive interpretation of human sexuality. Much of the official interpretation by Church authorities and quasi-official interpretation offered by some priests and nuns dealt with "should nots" and reflected a negative view of sexuality. In actual practice, however, people were often skeptical of an interpretation of God that said one sexual sin meant eternal damnation, at least when it applied to them or to someone they knew.

Thus, when a teenage boy died in an automobile accident, his friends dismissed the nun's comment that he would be in hell if he and his girlfriend had been aroused in their kissing the previous evening. So, too, divorce was wrong; but when some aunt who had been abandoned by her spouse later found a new mate, the relatives agreed "God understands, even if the Church doesn't." Premarital sex was wrong, but when a young woman became pregnant, she was not ostracized from the community. Necking and petting were condemned, but frequent confession provided ready forgiveness for all the offenses of a Saturday night date.

So it was that the hopeful world-view, short-circuited in the official and semi-official interpretations, was allowed to resurface in the personal interpretation. In St. Angela this third level of interpretation was encouraged by the attitude of many of the clergy and religious. The priests and nuns were creatures of their times and, as such, were not as open to the experience of the laity as we want religious leaders to be today. But in a period when everything had its place, they were in sufficient touch with the situation of the people they served to provide support for the search for meaning experienced by individuals and families. The myths and rituals of the common faith contributed to a sense of belonging, and the ministry of the parish allowed for an interpretation of the common faith that contributed to a positive world-view.

For families, this view of a place for everything contributed to an acceptance of roles with little questioning. Man was the head of the family (though, depending on the ethnic group, this headship might be much less than the male liked to think it was). Woman's place was in the home (even during the war few women in the parish worked). Children were taught the importance of the fourth commandment (and were offered forgiveness for their transgressions of it through frequent confession). Teenagers did not exhibit great identity crisis. In most instances, parents accepted their children with little concern about pushing them to be high achievers.

There was widespread support for acceptance of roles in the community because everyone shared common ideals about correct behavior. And the parish structure reinforced the belief that these roles were acceptable. Men and women's organizations were designed around the demands of the male-female roles. The school and high club assisted parents as they sought to pass on values to their children. The high club offered teenagers support as they tried to assimilate the values of the adult world.

The function of the high club in the lives of many of the teenagers is an example of how the parish functioned as a support group. There was a considerable pressure from peers to conform to expectations not always in agreement with parental values. When the group said it was acceptable to drink to excess, there was usually no way to escape the pressure of the group's attitude. The high club offered an opportunity for an acceptable adult (the priest moderator) to be in touch with the times when the group would be moving too far in its unorthodox behavior. He could then apply appropriate pressure to bring group members back in line. One priest moderator began establishing a good relationship with the young people during their grade school years. He was then viewed as a friend when they moved on to high school. Even though at times they found him a bit of an "old fogey" (especially when he didn't approve of drinking outside the gym during a high club dance), they were happy he was around to offer advice and support during the minor identity crisis and generation gap problems that occurred. They felt he liked them, and they liked him, so they accepted his legitimate loss of patience.

The myth, ritual and sacred place aspects of the parish also contributed to the sense of order in people's lives. Despite the present-day criticism of the static rituals of the past, these rituals played an important part in people's lives. More than likely this was because people put their own personal meaning into rituals that had grown static. Many of us still recall with warm feelings Benediction, Holy Week services, May Crownings, First Communions and other formal religious celebrations, not because the formal liturgy was so impressive, but because we attached our own meaning to these events.

St. Angela did not have many novenas, but there were Sunday afternoon Benedictions, the required mission, Stations of the Cross during Lent, and periodic special novenas. These, combined with five or six daily masses, gave people ample opportunity to participate in some form of liturgy. Since the Masses were in Latin, people were able to engage in their own private forms of worship (rosary novenas, St. Jude novenas, etc.) while attending the accepted Mass. The Church was open for visits until late each evening so those who wished to pray alone and undisturbed were able to do so. In addition, the open Church contributed to a strong, though unarticulated, sense that within the confines of the neighborhood there was a sacred place, serving as a reminder of the sacred in our lives.

But it was not the Church alone that served as a reminder of the sacred. All of the parish buildings played a role in reminding the people that they were part of a parish. Parish identity (and a reminder of the sacred) was reinforced each time a young person went over to play basketball, went to a meeting in the rectory basement, attended a high club dance, stopped in the convent to visit with a nun or joined in any of the many other activities connected with the parish plant. At St. Angela the buildings played a part in sending people out from the community with a Catholic identity.

The common faith and Catholic identity were also reinforced by the official rules and regulations of the Church. But when these were felt to be too oppressive, ways were found to circumvent them. The Italian men in the community were not bothered by their lack of attendance at Sunday Mass. So, too, when the Church said Sunday weddings could not be celebrated in conjunction with a Mass, the Italians, who enjoyed a tradition of Sunday weddings, simply had their weddings without a Mass. Though the non-Italians in the community considered this a less than legitimate way to celebrate a wedding, the Italians considered it important enough for them to be willing to put up with the lack of enthusiastic support from most of their non-Italian clergy and neighbors.

Obviously, during the 40's and 50's there was a minimal lay participation in the parish decision-making process, but neither was there an oppressive autocratic decision-making mentality on the part of the priests. Though there was little personal interaction between priests and lay people (it was all right for the priest to call a lay person by his or her first name, but priests were always addressed as "Father"), there was an openness on the part of the priests. With one or two exceptions they were "holy men who smiled." They were not excessively pious individuals, but they were the representatives of the holy in the community and, for the most part, they appeared happy with their chosen role. They communicated a feeling that life in the rectory was good. Large numbers of young men went to the seminary, usually in direct proportion to the level of contentment exhibited by the priests serving the community.

This brief review of the positive features of St. Angela during this time reveals that the parish ministers and parish activities combined to create a situation where people found support for their need for a common identity and a common faith. This support freed them to give personal and familial interpretations to reality. These interpretations were often closer to the faith of the Catholic tradition than many of the positions of the official Church at that time.

And so it was that the people of St. Angela were happy with their parish. Though they did not want to belong to another parish, it is only fair to observe that this was not because they felt that other parishes were that much different. They had a pride in St. Angela because it was "their" place. Anyone living on the West Side of Chicago at that time would have felt that all parishes gave the same feeling of identity. They would not have thought moving to another parish would be a disruptive experience. It simply meant moving from one Catholic community to another similar Catholic community. A parish with a "hell fire and brimstone" pastor might require some adjusting on the part of the new parishioner, but most people did not analyze their experience of parish. They simply assumed that the spirit of one parish would be easily translated to another.

New Leadership for the Local Church

That was certainly the case with the young people who had grown up in St. Angela during the 40's and 50's. They left St. Angela in the 60's never having considered what the parish meant to them, but expecting that their new parish would give the same support for a common faith. They expected to find a parish where there would be "a place for everything and everything in its place." They were not prepared for what would happen in many parishes when it became necessary to adapt to the new understandings of common faith and religious community evolving out of the analysis of the Church's relationship to the modern world.

Failure to recognize the way in which parish in the pre-Vatican II church was a supporter of a common faith and also a neighborhood left many religious leaders with little understanding of how to adapt the parish to the religious insights of the Second Vatican Council. Three common responses are the cause of much of the current readiness to dismiss parish as a viable religious institution. And none of these recognize the reasons for the success of parish in earlier periods.

First of all, there was the decision by some people in religious opinion-making circles that the immigrant parish model had been a failure and no geographical parish could possibly meet the religious needs of people in the transient modern world. New forms of religious community should be developed that would allow people to form community where they wanted it, not have to join a community on the basis of where they lived. Next, there were those who agreed that much of what had been the core of the immigrant parish was divisive and narrow. They felt that they could form a Christian community only if they could encourage the people to give up all the old religious practices. And finally, there were those who wanted to ignore the changes in both the world and the church that had caused the movement out of the fortress mentality of the pre-Vatican II church. They attempted to turn the parish into a fortress ruled over by the clergy, with the pastor continuing to talk about "my" parish and "my" word as final.

People from St. Angela who move into a parish with priests espousing any of these views soon become disheartened. When they encounter clergy who feel parish is a non-viable institution, they experience a questioning of the importance of their religious upbringing. When they are not given an opportunity to participate in the reformulation of the parish community, they turn off liberal priests who try to force new ideas on them whether they like them or not. They no longer feel a spirit of belonging to their parish. Still, most of these people feel they belong to a particular neighborhood (even though in the newer suburban areas they no longer use the term "neighborhood"). In parishes subjected to the automatic rule of rigid pastors, they also experience the loss of a feeling of religious community. They are part of the modern world to which the Council has spoken, and they are ready to be part of a new church, if they are only given the chance to understand it. They are not always specific about their discontent, but in each of these situations, the parish structure fails to encourage a sense of common faith springing from a religious tradition's response to the modern world. There is no place for everything; indeed, it seems there is a place for nothing and for no one.

Those who are fortunate enough to move to a place like Mary, Seat of Wisdom in suburban Park Ridge, Illinois, find themselves in a parish that, though quite different from St. Angela, still engenders the same spirit of parish they experienced in their youth. The story of this relatively new parish (celebrating its silver jubilee in 1980) is a story filled with myths.[1] As John Cusick, former associate pastor, comments, "There are so many myths about Mary, Seat of Wisdom and Bill Clark (the pastor) that soon it will be hard to tell the myth from the reality." But as Mircea Eliade maintains, myth makes people do what they ordinarily would not do. Part of the secret of the success of this parish as a post-Vatican II religious community is that the people there are doing the "impossible." They are making what many religious commentators have claimed an impossible task (celebrating religious community in a geographical parish) an exciting reality.

Just as their parents and grandparents before them, the people of Mary, Seat of Wisdom have a religious community where they feel they belong. As a relatively new community (the parish was founded in response to the growth of the Catholic population in Park Ridge where, until the mid-fifties, one parish had been sufficient for the Catholics of the then predominately Protestant community), there were few deep-rooted traditions to prevent an enthusiastic response to the challenges of the Second Vatican Council.

The call for active participation by the laity in their religious community has resulted in numerous organizations and groups. The sense of belonging is reinforced when people find themselves involved with fellow parishioners in one or more of these parish activities. The pluralism of religious interests and needs along with the diversity of social interests of the members of the parish has been responded to in a variety of ways. It is not an exaggeration to claim that at Mary, Seat of Wisdom there is something for everyone (or if there is not something right now, there is the opportunity to try to begin it soon).

People who are interested in liturgy may be part of the liturgy team, be one of the over one hundred lay ministers of the Eucharist, add their names to the large roster of lectors, commentators and leaders of song, join the high school guitar group that plays at the 9:45 Mass each Sunday, or volunteer to be part of the adult choir when it sings for special liturgies. Those who want to explore their faith in more depth than is possible at the Sunday liturgies have access to five Christian Family Movement groups, a Marriage Encounter group, small communities that meet regularly to read the bible and pray together, charismatic prayer groups, an Opus Dei group, a small group of men who meet with the priests to discuss a religious book one lunch hour a week, a large Ladies' Theology program now almost fifteen years old, and a smaller group of these women, who, along with the rectory staff, study during the summer with a systematic theologian from the major seminary (in the summer of 1980 they studied Edward Schillebeeckx's *Jesus*).

Over 400 adults and teenagers have participated in a weekend retreat program that grew out of a mission preached by Father Leo Mahon shortly after his return from Panama. Both the teenage and adult versions of this retreat attempt to help the clergy and laity explore together the implications of the vision of Jesus for the life of the parish community. As a result of this retreat movement there is an increased awareness on the part of the laity of the various ministerial roles they can perform. Ministers of Care have been trained to visit the local hospitals and nursing homes. A new Ministry to the Bereaved program has trained people, who have themselves suffered the loss of a loved one, to comfort the newly bereaved in a variety of ways. Participants in a bail bond project assist jailed persons who do not understand the details of release on bail. High school students for many years worked the Skid Row soup line one night a week. On Christmas morning many of the "graduates" of this program (even some who are out of college) still return to hand out gifts and a smile and song to the poor and homeless who come for a Catholic Charities Christmas dinner. During the summer of 1979 and 1980, groups of teenagers spent a week in an Appalachian parish helping on a building project and teaching bible classes.

Opportunities to assist in educational programs abound. Volunteers run the pre-school religion classes on Sunday morning, some parishioners teach in the parish school and in both the grade and high school level CCD programs. Mothers volunteer many hours as teacher's aides and assist with playground duty at lunch time. Adults lead the Junior Great Books program. There is an adult education committee that seeks to present programs on topics of particular interest in the parish. Parents of teenagers, encouraged by one of the parish priests, began an education/discussion program with the hope of fostering better communication between the two generations. The Over and Under Club (for those over and under retirement age) plans programs to assist its members with their specific problems.

There are numerous other activities that, while not specifically religious in nature, foster the sense of belonging important for a religious community. The parish council, the school board, the Home-School Association (similar to PTA), the youth group (high school age), the young adult group, the Council of Catholic Women, the women's guilds, the annual adult variety show in the Fall and the youth club variety show in the Spring, the summer volleyball program (in its ninth year in 1980 and attracting nearly 800 high school, college and young adult people four or five evenings a week in the parish gym), three or four parties sponsored by the guilds as well as the now annual New Year's Eve party, a women's club luncheon, a plant sale, an ice cream social, an annual family picnic and an annual Sunday brunch and auction fund raiser, along with "drop in and say hello" nights in the rectory when college people are home for school breaks all contribute to a sense of belonging on the part of those who participate in them.

And for many, belonging to Mary, Seat of Wisdom is especially important because it is a concerned and caring community. Even though suburbs such as Park Ridge do not usually consider themselves neighborhoods, the parish of Mary, Seat of Wisdom has managed to incorporate many of the positive features of the immigrant neighborhood into a suburban setting. Not only are the priests and religious concerned about the parishioners, but there is a spirit of concern for each other among the parishioners. When there is a new baby, an illness, or a death in the family, dinners magically appear for the family. When someone loses a job, there are offers of support in finding a new position and even offers of financial assistance to "tide the family over," silently made by some of the more financially secure members of the parish.

"Neighboring" also is evident in the amount of social time parish members spend with each other. In one survey it was indicated that four of the five couples some of the active parishioners socialize with are either members of the parish or live in the community. It is not at all unusual for the parish priests to stop in at several gatherings within the parish on a Saturday evening and to find that most of the people present at these gatherings are parishioners.

Belonging to Mary, Seat of Wisdom is so important that many parishioners, when they find they have outgrown their houses, will look at other houses only within the community. If a suitable house is not available, quite a few families have turned to room additions as a way of satisfying their space needs while remaining within the parish (there is very little vacant property in Park Ridge on which to build new homes). One family with ten children doubled the size of their house through an addition. Men have been known to turn down transfers and new job opportunities rather than uproot their families from the community. People who do move from the parish are often heard warning others not to make the same mistake. "You just don't realize what a good place you have, until you move into a parish like ours," is a not uncommon refrain from former parishioners.

So it is that we find the neighborhood/parish of Mary, Seat of Wisdom a natural outgrowth of the neighborhood/parish that most of the parishioners lived in when they were young. But since the understanding of church has changed dramatically over the years, the common faith, myths and rituals and rules and regulations of the pre-Vatican II parish have undergone a transformation in this modern parish.

The certitude that salvation is available to the individual soul through obedience to the laws of God and the Church and participation in the sacramental system is no longer the unifying theme of the common faith of the parish community. It would be a mistake, however, to think that diversity within the various groups in the parish is a sign that there is no unifying faith. Rather the diversity is an indication that people are finally acknowledging what had been a fact even among the immigrant communities—there are a variety of ways of living what it means to be a Catholic. There is an expectation that the religious leaders of the parish will continually present to the community a developing understanding of what it means to be a follower of Jesus in the present day. Leo Mahon's emphasis on the vision of the Kingdom preached by Jesus is the closest we can come to identifying what is the common faith of the parish.[2]

Though there are still some in the community who continue to look to the hierarchy to tell them what they have to do and believe to be a Catholic today, many people at Mary, Seat of Wisdom are searching for a way to incorporate their own experiences into the understanding of God preached by Jesus. In many respects this is not unlike the situation in earlier parishes where the level of personal interpretations was often closer to the basic beliefs of the Catholic faith than many of the official teachings of church authorities. The difference today is that people acknowledge that they are not always in agreement with church authority.

Much of the emphasis in the immediate post-Vatican II era was on active participation and social action, and Mary, Seat of Wisdom responded favorably to this challenge. The vision of a group of followers of Jesus' plan for the Kingdom has not yet developed a ritual where people find their spiritual life greatly enhanced by the liturgy. Although the overwhelming majority of parishioners are in favor of the new liturgy and are satisfied with the homilies, many feel a lack in their spiritual development. One layman summed up the feelings of some of the laity when he said the most pressing need of the parish now is "to develop a spirituality for the laity, a way in which we can find the encouragement to continue to follow the vision, even when our day-to-day life drags us down." Certain liturgical celebrations, especially during Advent, Christmas, Lent and Easter and for special events such as weddings, funerals, confirmations, etc., do encourage a feeling of celebration, but there is still much to be done to integrate the Sunday liturgies and the experiences of the people. The positive note is that this need is recognized and many people (both clergy and laity) are trying to improve the situation.

The parish plant at Mary, Seat of Wisdom continues the tradition of the earlier parishes. It is the center of the parish community, and the many functions that occur there are a reminder to those who participate in them that they do belong to Mary, Seat of Wisdom, that they have a Catholic identity. Hardly a night goes by that the gym, the Meet and Talk Room (the substitute for the rectory basement when the rectory has no basement), the parish library, some of the classrooms and one or more of thé priest's rooms are not the site of some activity. Even those young people who no longer participate in Sunday liturgies (much to the consternation of their parents) are going to have memories of positive experiences associated with Mary, Seat of Wisdom.

Role support in a world where it is no longer true that "there is a place for everything and everything in its place" is extremely difficult. At Mary, Seat of Wisdom, support for a specific model of wife-husband roles is no longer possible. There are too many different models of family life within the community. Support is localized within specific age and friendship groups. Young mothers with small children help each other deal with the problems they are facing while middle-age mothers with their last child in high school are moving together into new dimensions of the role of wife and mother. And men at all ages find themselves more involved in child-care than most of their fathers were, but still rather unsure of where they fit in the transitions going on in family life today.

Where support is more evident at Mary, Seat of Wisdom is in the parent-child relationship. Parents are offered assistance beginning with a pre-Baptism visit to help prepare them for their role as Christian parents. Through various levels of grade school and continuing into the teenage years, parents are offered programs dealing with both the religious and social development of the child. The teenager at Mary, Seat of Wisdom has access to a Youth Group that offers support similar to those at St. Angela. At a time when more and more people are looking to the family to give them their greatest emotional satisfaction, Mary, Seat of Wisdom is turning its attention to the communication problems within the family. Various approaches for meeting the needs of family members at different periods of their family life cycles are being discussed and experimented with.

Since the overwhelming majority of the highschoolers attend the local public high school, those who do not participate in the youth group do not have the same strong parish identification that was found on the West Side of Chicago. What these young people do have, however, is a model of parents who are actively involved in a busy parish. They also have a model of a religious community where clergy and laity are working together toward a goal of living a Christian life.

Leadership in a post-Vatican II parish like Mary, Seat

of Wisdom, is obviously quite different than that at St. Angela. Laity participate, through the parish council and school board, in any major decision affecting the life of the parish. There is a warm relationship between the people and the priests and religious leaders of the parish. The rectory is an open house where all are welcome, even beyond the doors to the previously "private, priest-only" corridors and rooms of the second floor. Since 1970, the rectory has been, in the words of John Cusick, "a fun place to live." And this fact has not escaped the notice of the parishioners.

The leadership style of the pastor, Father William Clark, known affectionately by all as "Uncle Bill," is based on love and trust. The rest of the parish staff (two associate pastors, a woman religious pastoral associate, and a deacon) find this love and trust allows them to work easily with each other and to be open to the people of the community.

The laity consider the priests their friends. They have a deep affection and love for "Uncle Bill." As one man observed, "You might get mad at one of the others, but you never get mad at Uncle Bill, even when you might not like what he's doing." It is Father Clark's openness to all people (even those with whom he has disagreements about the proper Christian response to a particular problem) that provides a unifying force among the diverse groups within the parish. He uses what John Cusick calls the "Jesus Method" in dealing with situations that he considers contrary to the vision of Catholicism. He criticizes what is happening, but always remains open to the people involved. As one associate pastor observed, "I learned from him how to temper my outrage so it gets to the content and not at the person."

Obviously, a more detailed reflection on the story of Mary, Seat of Wisdom would reveal that it has some shortcomings. We do, however, realize, as we examined the experience of the parish, that it has the potential for dealing with most of the problems which have not been addressed. Father Clark's deeply religious sense along with his love and concern for people has set a tone that motivates the other clergy and the laity to want the parish to work. In the case of Mary, Seat of Wisdom, as in the case of St. Angela, the parish does work at meeting the needs of its members.

When personal experience tells us that some parish experiences are good, we ask if these are merely flukes or are there some sociological and/or theological reasons why local community might also be religious community. Should we dismiss the significance of St. Angela as merely a creature of its time having no connection with religious community in our contemporary world? Is Mary, Seat of Wisdom simply an instance of upper middle class white Americans who are trying to hold onto something whose day is really over? Or should these stories lead us to examine the role of local community in human experience to determine if it is a natural base for religious community? Should we wonder if this base continues to exist in the modern world?

The interdisciplinary method of this study begins with reflection on experience (the story of two parishes) and now moves to the insights of the social sciences in order to determine how our experimental bias toward local church is substantiated by a scientific understanding of human interaction.

CHAPTER 2

Sociological Perspective of the Local Church

THE myth of "The Unconnected Person" influences much of the conversations of theologians, religious leaders, and ministers whenever they turn to the topic of local church. The myth goes something like this:

> With the advent of mass media, instant communication, rapid transportation, the emergence of world community and all the other future shock phenomena, men and women have undergone profound change. Not only are we no longer the rooted creatures we once were, but, as isolated individuals and isolated family units, we live an anomic, unconnected existence. A great many of us (those who do not look at census data might say as many as one-half) are constantly on the move and find ourselves hastily integrated into rapidly changing communities in which the focus may change but the community structures go undiminished. And for all of us the "real" world (that is, the important world) is the competitive, career-oriented world where the decisions that really affect society are made.

It really does not matter that most of the people having these conversations do not know many (if, in fact, they know any) of these unconnected people. The fact that perhaps one portion of the myth might apply to a few people they know seems to give validity to the entire myth. Much of the pop sociology that works itself into best-seller paperbacks supports this myth and lends credence to a belief in the demise of the continuing presence of a sense of rootedness, and of the importance of local community, hearth, home, family, neighborhood and church. Mary, Seat of Wisdom can be dismissed as a fluke, a place where people have failed to catch up with the "modern world," another form of Catholic ghetto that will soon fade from the scene.

This myth has its roots in the modernization fallacy that has become part of the collective preconsciousness of the north Atlantic world. Our approach to a positive sociological view of local religious community will first refute the modernization model of human behavior and the turn to two different traditions—the animal behavior studies of the sociobiologist and ethologist and the work on the importance of neighborhoods done by some of the better members of the so-called Chicago school—to support our position that local community plays a critical role in the lives of contemporary humans. After we have examined why it is that humans form local communities, we will examine the process of socialization that occurs in local communities.

Modernization Fallacy

The modernization model for human behavior (which we take to mean that the changes of the last several hundred years have resulted in the emergence of a radically new kind of human consciousness) is a very attractive model since it does fit very well some of the data that are immediately obvious to everyone. We know that mass media, instant communication, and rapid transportation have introduced changes that could never have been imagined by our grandparents (our frequent trips to the lands our immigrant forebears never saw again after their departure for America is but one example). The myth is reinforced by all the evolutionary theories—Marxist, Comtist, Darwinian and Christian. Even the most sophisticated social scientist is apt to maintain that bureaucratization is the inevitable result of science and technology since the two have been linked historically. And other historical linkages seem to support the modernization myth.

Talcott Parsons and his colleagues and students have provided the most elaborate description of the modernization phenomenon. The broad line of their argument is that the Reformation freed the individual from the rigid controls of medieval society; and the newly independent and mobile individuals began to explore the far reaches of the globe, the internal depths of the personality, the complexities of the world, and the various possibilities of the new scientific knowledge that their explorations made possible. A multiplier effect set in and knowledge, technology, mobility and innovation accelerated the speed of development. New institutions emerged to make use of knowledge, technology and freedom. They rapidly differentiated themselves, acquiring more and more specific functions. State bureaucracies, mercantile organizations, and eventually manufacturing and transportation corporations emerged to handle functions that either had not existed previously or had been taken care of by the Church and family in much less elaborate fashion. The family began to focus specifically on the provision of emotional satisfaction to the spouses and on the socialization of the children, yielding virtually all of its productive and economic functions to the new corporations. The Church gradually limited its role to dealing with ultimate issues, yielding its legal, economic, and welfare roles to new institutions or to the growing state bureaucracies.

Add to this the new differentiation of roles and the divison of labor within the family and we find that the husband became the specialist in abstract, task-oriented leadership in the family while the wife became the socio-emotional specialist. The child was thus forced to internalize two kinds of parents—the abstract parent and the loving parent. The tension caused by the two-parent internalization led to a personality with both the need and the ability to break even more decisively with the traditions of the past. Modern man, "The Unconnected Person," was born.

With its "evolutionary" and "progressive" character, representing the wave of history and the natural working out of forces of development for a fuller and freer human life, the modernization myth flatters our pride. We are in the advance guard, better than those who went before us, the way for those who will come after us. Our policies, programs and ideologies must be the best because they are the inevitable result of the historical process. The crux of our critique of this model relies on the work of the "rediscoverers of primary groups" who question the *terminus ad quem* of modernization, the work of historical demographers who question the *terminus a quo* of it and the political scientists who study the "new nations."

Beginning with Elton Mayo's Hawthorne studies in the late 1920's, a massive amount of evidence has been assembled to indicate that the primordial, the informal, the primary not only survive but keep the large corporate bureaucracies running. It was the friendship group on the

Hawthorne assembly line that determined the productivity standard. It was the small combat squad held together by loyalty to the father-figure noncom officer that kept the modern army going. Marketing decisions, the use of new drugs by doctors and of innovative agricultural methods by farmers take place not in interactions between an isolated individual and the mass media but in small informal friendship groups in which various "opinion leaders" became the key persons in diffusing innovation and impelling decisions. The majority of American families still live within a mile of at least one grandparent, and siblings and cousins are still the people with whom visits are most frequently exchanged for most of us. The world is not on a pilgrimage from the particularist to the universalist; it is rather a combination of both.

Of course, things have changed. We have a much larger number of formal, stylized, specific relationships, but not, as some would have us think, at the expense of the informal, casual, diffuse ones of the past. Rather, the number of human relationships has simply increased. Also some relationships, such as marriage and family ties, do not have the compelling physical depth they used to have for our ancestors in the "premodern" world. Divorce did not occur and leaving one's family for another country or continent was for all practical purposes to die. Today, divorce is possible and telephone and air travel reduce the trauma of leaving home. Yet one could make the case that the psychological depth of some relationships is much greater today and that far greater demands for intimacy and vulnerability are placed upon us—along with promises of far greater rewards—than we have developed the personal skills to respond to.

The historical demographers, who dig back into parish

registers, county archives, and other ancient and musty sources of data to reconstruct the vital statistics and family structures of previous ages, have had an absolutely devastating impact on all broad and general theories about what Europe looked like in the time between the thirteenth and the eighteenth centuries. Family size, age at marriage, living arrangements, life expectancies, mobility—all varied up and down in those centuries, depending on such factors as agricultural productivity, internal peace, disease epidemics, and the ebb and flow of technological innovations. The picture that emerges, though rich, complex, dense and fascinating, does not fit any simple unidimensional, unidirectional model of social change. More important, for our critique of modernization, we find that private property and the nuclear family—both thought to be the "results" of modernization—have existed in Western Europe as far back as the demographic researchers can go.

The greatest impetus to our modern era was not the revolution in ideas, nor was it the development of industrial technology. Rather it was an enormous population expansion that occurred in Europe in the early to middle 1700's and persisted in Europe until the middle to end of the 1800's. A number of factors contributed to the expansion, including the development of natural immunities to infectious disease parasites, the warming of the climate after a hundred years of a "little ice age," the absence of foreign invasions, the development of international and intercontinental trade and the development of crude but effective vaccination against smallpox. All of these changes enabled people to live longer and caused the migration of large numbers of landless peasants from farms to cities, without which the industrial expansion could not have been possible. Other effects included migration across the sea to the new World; the first (and probably only "real") sexual revolution with the breakup of the strong moral control of preindustrial peasant society over young people; more concern for children on the part of parents (when only one out of two infants survived to adulthood, parents tended to restrain their emotional investment in children); and eventual development of effective means of population control. Whatever change in consciousness we find in modern humans is probably the result of the fact that people lived long enough to acquire a new consciousness (something they had not done for prolonged periods in the past).

A final source of doubt concerning the evolutionary theory of modernization is found in the research done by historically-oriented sociologists on the actual modernization process that is going on in the "new nations" that have emerged since 1945. The work of Joseph Elder, Manning Nash, Richard Lambert, as well as political scientists, Lloyd and Suzanne Rudolph and anthropologist, Clifford Geertz, indicates that "modern man" is not that much different from our ancestors but that we have acquired some new skills, perspectives and experiences along with a longer life expectancy and greater social and geographical mobility. People in the emerging countries studied by these scholars are a mixture of "traditional" and "modern," with the traditional by no means minimized. The modern builds on the traditional rather than replacing it.

Thus, the sociologists of the primary group, with their rediscovery of the persistence of *Gemeinschaft* in the modern world, the demographic historians in their rediscovery of the nuclear family and private property at the beginning of modernization and the social scientists who analyze "developing" nations find a marvelous combination of modernity and tradition intertwined with one another. All three strike a shattering blow to the modernization myth.

Sociobiology and Ethology

As a result of long-standing disagreements between social scientists and biologists, much of sociological theory during the past fifty years developed with little, if any, recognition of the importance of the biological component of human nature (an analysis of the reasons for this and of the need for a reapproachment on the part of social scientists is summarized in Alice Rossi's article "A Biosocial Perspective on Parenting," *Daedalus,* Spring, 1977). The modernization myth as well as the myth of "The Unconnected Person" developed from the disregard of the implications of our bodiliness on every human activity. Our consciousness is expressed through our bodies and until social scientists are willing to admit the implications of this fact, we will always be subjected to fallacies similar to that of "The Unconnected Person."

The important point for our present purposes to be learned from the ethologists, the sociobiologists and the comparative primatologists, is that humankind is an animal species that does occupy territory. We are not archangels. We have yet to acquire the capacity to move with the speed of light or the speed of thought. We have length and width and height. We cannot be in two places at the same time (and those of us who spend a good deal of our time commuting back and forth between various places soon begin to realize that our bodies do not respond well to frequent changes). Our human territoriality is "like" animal territoriality but also somewhat different from it. We can give up our territories and move to others much more readily than can our chimpanzee and baboon cousins. At the same time, the ability to reflect upon the fact that our "turf" is ours makes our possible instinct of territoriality notably different from that of the other primates. We do not need to postulate any genetic predetermination to account for resistance to being pushed off our turf. We human animals may defend our turf for the perfectly reasonable (to us) motivation that we like it, that we have our money tied up in it, and that our friends live there, and not because of a biological imperative. Whether we be instinctually territorial or not is of less importance, finally, than that our status as embodied beings makes us subject to the law of inertia.

Furthermore, we are a highly social species, inclined to long term relationships with our mates and offspring, for whom the same inertia laws apply as apply to us. Alone of all the primates, the human species has a powerful proclivity for pairbonding. Indeed, biologists and primatologists now contend that much of what is distinctive in human sexuality (constant sexual availability of women, constant preoccupation with matters sexual in both sexes, the affection that normally attaches to human sex, sustained duration of human sexual intercourse) are not necessary for primate procreation and/or reproduction. These characteristics exist, rather, to create and sustain the emotional bond between the male and female hominid. Indeed, some of these scientists argue that this pairbond, found often in lower life forms like birds, is rare in primates and had to come into existence in the prehuman hominids as an essential condition for evolution as *homo sapiens*. Tied down in time and place by our nature as an embodied creature, humankind is even more tied down by our nature as a pairbond forming creature. You may be able to move around a lot yourself, but what are you going to do about your family?

Animals that we are, with genetic and biological propensities and programming, we are also remarkably flexible creatures capable of enormous programming by our culture and also of very substantial self-programming. We may tend to identify with one place but very early in human existence we learned to roam whenever it was necessary to roam to survive. We tried to bring our family and our friends with us but when that was impossible, we went by ourselves and returned home whenever we could. Neither determined to a specific place, nor free from a need for a "place of our own," the human animal is in one paradoxical sense more territorial than other animals. If our attachments to a place of our own is not necessarily genetic or biological, it can become far more important psychologically and emotionally to us than it is to any other creature. We find the work of these scientists leading us to reject the territorial imperative and substitute in its place a territorial propensity, rooted in our nature as embodied, pairbonding, friendship-forming creatures.

Neighborhoods

When we turn from the sociobiological to the sociological and the sociocultural, we are on much safer grounds. While it is not clear how much of our social behavior is biologically programmed, it is certainly clear that there are powerful social and cultural dynamics at work in human society that lead us to form local communities of one kind or another. Contrary to those who say that "neighborhood" played an important role for Catholic immigrants but that with the move to the suburbs the neighborhood ceased to be important, the empirical evidence indicates that some suburban neighborhood parishes, like Mary, Seat of Wisdom, are far more vigorous and dynamic than ethnic immigrant parishes were. In part this might be because the immigrant parish was the product of social and economic necessity while the suburban parish is much more a community of free association and intimacy, created by free contact. The dormitory suburbs are not merely places where people sleep and conceive their children. They are also places of intense social, recreational, and sometimes cultural and political relationships. They are places to which one escapes for peace and relaxation with one's own kind and one's closest friends when one finally gets away from the "rat race" of the "real" world.

Local community has an enormous durability in the human condition. The styles and patterns of it may change, precisely because humankind is such a flexible, self-programmable creature. Some humans may have need for and dispositions toward local community that exceed the needs and dispositions of others. There are marginal members of the suburban community and the suburban religious community; so too there were marginal members of the urban immigrant community and the rural American small town. Even those citizens who have opted for the mobile transient life desperately search for local community, however transitory their stay might be.

Why the durability of local communities? Humankind is, as is evident from observation, a cooperative and gregarious relationship-forming creature. For reasons of psychological and emotional convenience, we tend to form relationships with those who are most like ourselves and for reasons of physical convenience we tend to form them with those who happen to be physically closest to us. Thus we seek out our "own kind of people" in the place where we live or even choose the place where we live in part because there are already some of our own kind of people (however defined) in that place. A "neighborhood" is nothing more than a physical place where one is in association with one's own kind of people—some of whom have doubtless become or have been discovered as one's own kind of people only after living in physical proximity with them for a certain period of time. The neighborhood, like the family, then probably antedates the emergence of *homo sapiens* and will persist in some form as long as there are *homo sapiens.* The forms neighborhoods may take are multitudinous because humankind can choose from a wide variety of possible interaction patterns. But because the pattern changes, it does not follow that "neighborhood" or "family" is declining, but only that it is changing. The local community is even more important for humankind when it happens to be the place where one's spouse and children live and where one's children are raised. Thus, for reasons of physical as well as psychological convenience and because of concern about spouse and children, we human animals tend to be concerned about, committed to, and attached to the local community in which we find ourselves.

Thus we come to the concept of the "defended neighborhood" introduced by Jerry Suttles of the so-called Chicago school, in part to refute the "Territorial Imperative" argument of Desmond Morris and Robert Ardery. A neighborhood, Suttles concedes, is by definition a place to be defended, but not for reasons of genetic programming. It is rather a place where (a) our family and our friends live, and (b) where in the massive urban checkerboard we find "our kind of people" with whom we feel "safe." For these reasons our neighborhoods are important to us and we need not be racist to want to protect and defend them. For, if the neighborhood is taken away, we no longer have a place to come home to. We have lost a network of relationships with our own kind of people. We have been deprived of a locus where there are common values, common assumptions, established patterns of relationships, and psychological and often physical safety.

Suttles' concept of the "defended neighborhood" is developed in response to the "Territorial Imperative" pop ethology and assumes an urban checkerboard in which many if not most of the squares are either psychologically and/or physically dangerous and only one square is both psychologically and physically safe. The concept illustrates the broader truth we are examining here: Humankind—granting always wide flexibility and broad variations of behavior—is prone to seek out a place of its own and then to become attached to that place. Any philosophical anthropology or religious programming (to say nothing of urban, political or social planning) which ignores this is candidly asking for trouble.

American Catholic humankind is especially disposed to such "localism." While it is easy to find things wrong with the immigrant neighborhood parish (and equally easy to idealize it), it must still be reckoned on balance one of the more successful social innovations to new circumstances ever devised in the history of Roman Catholicism. Our intelligentsia and literati have ridiculed it—perhaps because they had to escape from it or thought they had to escape from it to be free to do their work—but the vast majority of American Catholics found it a more benign adaptation, evidenced by the way in which they tried to create something like it once they left behind the old neighborhood.

So it seems that it is utterly frivolous and self-indulgent to proclaim the slogan "create community." Clergy do not come into a situation in which there are isolated, rootless and anomic individuals without any existing patterns of relationships and then by proclaiming the gospel and convening the eucharistic assembly, call community into being. Juxtapose human animals in almost any imaginable set of circumstances and they will create their own community. And when these communities are where people live with their spouses and children, the socialization process within the community becomes of paramount importance.

Local Community and Socialization

Socialization is a fancy word for getting people to do what we want them to do at an early age. The primary socialization of the individual is in the family of origin and the parents play the key role. Subsequent socialization occurs in the school and the neighborhood and peer group and the family of choice, but the basic directions tend to be determined in the first socialization experience in the family of origin. However, the construction of sociality does not end with the parents' interaction with the child, but continues as each of us grows from childhood to adulthood through the various socializing agencies with which we come in contact.

The specific groups which concern us at the local community level are the family, school, ethnic groups, religious groups, and other voluntary associations. These groups act interdependently and their socializing influences are overlapping, which makes rigorous analysis of their impact difficult. However, it is possible to speculate on their function in the local community and perhaps from that speculation we will be able to differentiate them one from the other.

The first function which these socializing groups perform at the local level is that of "bonding." Bonding is that aspect of human behavior which ties us together, or to a specific place, or to a specific group of people. It is the sense of belonging which is so important in human development. In our earliest years we have a need to belong to a family; as we grow older we have a need to belong to a group of people, a place, a neighborhood, whatever. The socialization process is another name for our conviction that the bonding is worthwhile. We need to believe that this is a good place to be, that these are good people to come from, that these are good friends to be with. This need is very strong in human beings and when it is not fulfilled there is usually some characterological disruption.

Another function which these groups all perform is to encourage within the individual the internalization of some set of values. They may be values about what is a good boy or girl, values about how family is to behave, values about how outsiders are to be treated, or any number of other rule, norm and value messages. The socialization process, though internalization, helps us convince ourselves that our values are worth holding onto and translating one to the other.

A third factor which characterizes the function of all these socializing agencies is the persistence of the local community, and of course the persistence of the specific socializing institutions as well. None of these groups are in the business of going out of business and they have all been around for a long time. Socialization deals directly with the issue of permanence and longevity in human life and the notion that the local community and the socializing agencies within it are connected to similar communities and agencies which existed in a former time is a very important part of the socialization process.

In the remaining section of this chapter we will examine the socialization process as it relates to the life cycle and to specific value systems. There are many different ways to characterize the life cycle but to simplify things we will consider three phases: childhood, adulthood, and the transition between them.

The basic issue in childhood for the individual is the question of whether or not one can trust the parents. The neighborhood analogy is whether or not one can trust the community. What is likely to happen to you in this neighborhood? Are the people here friendly or not? Do the kids want to play with me or not? These are the kinds of questions which are raised in the first stages of the life cycle and essentially they are questions of trust. Just as the family may provide something of a model of reality for the growing child, so the community can provide something of a model of the cosmos for the growing child. As the child begins to explore outside of him or herself, one of the first experiences is that of the surrounding people and geography within which the child's family exists. It would seem logical to assume that all kinds of messages about the nature of reality are being given to the child at this time and the message that comes from a healthy, vital, questioning community would be very different from one that comes from a fearful, isolated community or one that is simply dull. It would also seem that very different messages are given to a child in a community which has existed in one place for some long period of time than in one which is newly built or one which has the earmark of transition as being its major characteristic. Children require stability in the major adult relationships with which they interact and there is no reason to suspect that they require any less stability in their neighborhood context.

People who are in the transition stage between childhood and adulthood also depend on their local community or neighborhood for many symbolic messages. At this stage of life one's friends and family are almost equally important, and the social milieu which inhabits one's school is not far behind. The basic question which is being asked by the individual in this transition stage is who am I and what am I to do with my life, and it would seem likely that a lively, functioning community is the best place within which to ask that question. Within such a community the adolescent has role models to help decide the future course of his or her life. The local community is also the place where the adolescent learns many lessons which will be activated later on in life. This is a time for learning about friendship and trust and loyalty in a way that will either stay with the person or will vanish. The transition between childhood and adulthood is a move from a state of dependence and family to a state of independence and creating one's own family; it is paralleled by a move from a small, isolated circle of reality to a larger context of reality and this move happens within the local community. The adolescent who cannot relate successfully to his local community will have a very hard time relating to the larger issues which he or she will have to face in the world in later life.

Adulthood can be defined as that portion of the life cycle during which the person achieves some peace with who one is and what one does. This frequently represents another aspect of the socialization process and that is the secondary socialization phase of marriage. Marriage can be termed as the secondary socialization phase because the spouses tend to reeducate each other and attempt to internalize certain values in each other which the relationship needs to continue. There is also socialization in the work place and socialization in the home which happens once the independence status of adulthood is reached. The issue for the local community is whether or not it supports or criticizes these various aspects in the life cycle which the adult is entering into. For example, with regard to marriage, more and more pressures and expectations are being placed on marriages, yet it is not clear that marriages are being supported in the local community in the way they might be. Whereas the salient issues for the child and for the adolescent going through the transition period are learning issues, the salient issue for the adult is essentially a survival issue. Will the relationship survive, will success at work survive, will sanity in the home survive? These seem to be the questions adults frequently ask themselves.

The local community is the ground in which all of these processes occur. The relationship between the local community and the socialization process, at whatever stage of the life cycle, is reciprocal. The process affects the community and the community affects the process. This reciprocity is important in the kind of insight produced in the local community because the way in which we achieve meaning in life is reciprocal. We shape events and events in turn shape us.

The value socialization process within the local community can be organized by focusing on several different topic areas which seem to be common to most small communities. The process which attempts to promote the internalization of these specific values is an informal process consisting of questions and subleties rather than the formal training programs or anything of that sort. Many of these values are similar to one's imperative in the family and in all probability have their basis in early family socialization which is clearly the most important aspect of the process; however, each of these value areas is specifically related to the neighborhood or the local community and therefore carries specific internalized messages about the nature of reality as defined in the context of the local community.

The value-topics which we are going to discuss are respect, turf, world-view, hopefulness, and self-actualization. These topics do not exhaust the potential values which exist in a community and into which people need to be socialized, but they are representative of the larger categories of these value areas and they lend themselves to a discussion of the way in which individual values can be converted into collective value-topics within the local community.

Respect, for example, is a two-way street. People need to internalize a respect for their community and for the story that is represented within the community, and at the same time they need to internalize a demand within themselves that others respect their story and what it represents. Story, in this case, is another word for the ethos and the mythos of the local community—the properties which make it a special place in the minds of its residents as well as in the minds of those outside the community. People want their story to be taken seriously by others which means they want the history of their community and the traditions and the heritages and the values to be respected by other people. This doesn't necessarily mean that people have to agree with the values but we want others to have the sense that our story is as good as theirs. In order for this to happen, the story must be told within the community frequently. Children must hear the tales of the heritage spoken in the home and they must see them lived out within the community. They must also hear the demand for respect repeated within the community. It is good for children to believe that they come from a special and gifted place in the world and, contrary to conventional wisdom, this does not necessarily produce elitism or insularity. Self-respect can be taught in the home but respect for the story can only be taught within the community context.

Another element of the value structure of the community is a sense of ownership which is sometimes called a sense of turf. Although this word was originally used to describe the sense of control that youth gangs had over specific geographic areas, it has been used with more and more frequency to describe the sense of ownership, loyalty, bonding, etc. which people have specific to a certain place. The community analogy is that not only is there a specific community story but that that story takes place in a specific geographic reality. The sense of turf is analogous to the religious symbol of sacred space, in the sense that one's turf is where one finds peace and the time and space to contemplate the story and to evaluate one's own life. The local community is frequently endowed with a sense of the sacred by the fixation of parish names on geographic territories. "Being from St. Angela" reflected not only a geographic reality but a connection between the community sense of story and the religious sense of sacred which coexists in the same physical space. While this is obviously not true in all communities it is probably more true in most communities than outsiders are aware.

A third general value which is imparted through local community socialization processes is the world-view, both in an individual and in a collective sense. Internal world-view is that model of reality which we carry around with us to help us interpret the things that happen to us, and to make sense out of our surroundings. The collective sense of world-view is that model of reality which is held in common by the members of a specific community. Regarding the socialization function, the most interesting aspect of this value area is the way in which the collective sense of a world-view impinges and forms a context for the individual world-views of the members of the community. This is a very difficult subject to be concrete about, but for the sake of an example let us say that there is a community which has as part of its world-view the definition of itself as a predominantly Catholic community. If there is a specific Catholic style of coalition building and problem solving, it is then likely that this self-defined Catholic community would have a different world-view about solving community problems than some other geographic entity which had a different sort of heritage.

Another example is to be found in the places in which young people like to congregate. In some communities young people are more likely to use park facilities, for example, than church facilities; while in other communities, church parking lots and yards are the appropriate places to congregate rather than public park lands. What's the difference? One could speculate that the concept of church as represented by the building and the land plays a different part in the lives of the one group of young people than the other, and therefore in the lives of the members of the communities. It seems possible to find community expressions of various world-views if one looks hard enough, and once found, these expressions become evidence of the kind of value socialization that goes on in the general community context.

Hopefulness is defined as the conviction that good is slightly stronger than evil, or alternatively the conviction that one will ultimately survive even though it might be close. Although this is a component of a world-view according to some typologies, it also seems to be an important enough value to be treated by itself in this discussion. While it seems true that families are the particular purveyors of the attitude of hopefulness or whatever its alternative might be, it also seems to be the case that some communities are more hopeful than others. A hopeful community, in its elemental sense, would be one that believes in its own survival, and one in which that belief is contagiously transmitted to the residents of the community. Communities which have strong links to the past and which carry their traditions with them as they move through time would seem to be likely candidates for hopeful communities. The message that an individual would internalize while growing up in such a community is that survivability is possible, whether it be values or communities. The impact of this message on people's lives is an unknown factor, but it can be hypothesized that those who grow up in a community which espouses survivability as a characteristic are themselves likely to be better equipped to face tragedies, obstacles, and various kinds of tests as they go through life.

The last value area to be discussed is that of self-actualization or, as it has become known in the community organization field, "empowerment." Self-actualization or empowerment, otherwise known as a sense of efficacy, is the sense within persons that they have some power or control over their own destiny, and the collective analogy is that the residents of the community have some sense that they can get things done when they need them. There are many examples of communities which have convinced themselves that they could have an impact on the political and social context within which they exist and have then gone on to organize and have such an impact. Whether it be the blocking of a building they don't like or lobbying for a park or a facility which they think they need, such activities are fairly commonplace in American community life. Just as an individual needs to have the sense that he or she can break out of a mold and form their own future, so a community has to have the sense that it can control its own destiny. The value of self-actualization, whether internalized in the individual or in the collective community, is the result of socialization processes at both levels.

The value areas of the type discussed in this section are the intangibles in community analysis. Why is it that one community succumbs to the urban developer's bulldozer and another community of similar socio-demographic nature successfully resists development which it does not want? Why are some communities able to cope with rising crime rates better than others, independent of their socio-economic status? Why are some communities able to support, maintain and demand high quality education while others wait patiently for their schools to collapse? There are many sociological and cultural factors at work in these kinds of problems, but the intangible factor has to do with the value socialization which has taken place within the community, both on the individual and collective levels.

Thus we find that not only are today's men and women not unconnected persons, but that most of them live in neighborhoods where their development process as well as value socialization takes place. We have used the term neighborhood interchangeably with local community because it is one of the more common names by which we call the local groupings that we are interested in. Not all people live in neighborhoods (although Suttles' definition would lead us to argue that any local community could be called neighborhood and everyone belongs to some degree to some form of local community), but almost all people have lived in neighborhoods at one time or another, or if not, they wish they did.

The persistence of neighborhoods and the persistence of interest in neighborhoods (a territorial propensity we found rooted in our natures as embodied, pair-bonding, friendship-forming creatures) undoubtedly has a message for those of us trying to address religious issues. So, too, some of the socialization during life cycles and value socialization are religious in nature, if not specifically then at least generically.

Before examining the place of the local church in the Catholic systematic theology we need to turn to a consideration of how local community functions as a symbol of Sacred Space and of the function of religious symbols in local community socialization. Both of these topics pave the way for a better appreciation of the process of religious development in the local church.

CHAPTER 3

Religious Development in the Local Community

WHILE our sociological analysis, with its positive view of the significance of local community, supports the experience of parishioners in Mary, Seat of Wisdom who want a place where they belong and a place where they and their children receive support for the challenges of everyday life, the critic of local parish might still claim that we do not need a parish for this. People can find a place of their own and experience the socialization process without having any input from a religious community. As one cleric observed, "Belonging to a garden club could do as much for you people [he was talking to a parishioner of Mary, Seat of Wisdom] as belonging to the parish."

This denial of the importance of a local level religious community interacting with the other local communities ignores the importance of Sacred Space in human existence, the religious issues that surface in the socialization process and the process of religious encounter in individual and community lives. The neighborhood parish recognizes the religious dimension of local community and, though not always in a self-conscious manner, responded to the challenge to religious leadership found in local community. Our cleric with the garden club comment did not want to accept the challenge to him to lead people through the process of religious encounter.

Our analysis of the process of religious encounter begins with an examination of the materials on Sacred Time and Sacred Space derived from the history of religions and, in particular, from Mircea Eliade. We follow this with an analysis of the use of symbolic language in local community and of socialization and the interaction between specifically religious symbols and those that often appear to have little or no religious significance. We conclude with an outline of the process of religious encounter and suggestions of some implications this process has for local religious community.

Local Community and Sacred Space

Approaching this topic from the view of a "Secular Theory of Religion," we maintain that humankind has the propensity to hope, a capacity to experience grace, and the need (widely variable) to intermittently reinforce that hope through an experience of grace.[1] We further contend that the propensity to hope, the capacity to experience grace and the symbolization of that experience so that it may be articulated to oneself and shared with others are all activities of the pre-conscious or the creative imagination or the agent intellect or the mytho-poetic faculty or whatever else you want to call it. We also contend that there are certain pictures or images floating around in the memory—constantly being scanned by the agent intellect—that are especially important to us and especially powerful (sky, moon, sun, water, sexual differentiations, etc.) and that are, therefore, especially prone to serve as articulation of our experiences of graces. Local community is one of these symbols.

Hence, certain places representing a local community in one way or another tend to become externalizations and concretizations of the symbol Sacred Space. Following the notion that everything must be sacramental with a small s in order that some things may be sacramental with a large S, we contend that all places and every space is potentially revelatory, a potential occasion for an experience of grace. But especially liable to both occasion and articulate such experiences are those spaces that are the local community and particularly those central spaces that seem to quintessentially represent the local community (in Chicago: the Daley Civic Center, 100th and Longwood; in other places: The Piazza Santa Maria in Trastevere, the "hill" in St. Louis, etc., etc.). There are some places, in other words, that precisely because they are *our* place, *our* local community, or *our* local community par excellence, are especially likely to be both sacrament and sacramental symbol (by which we mean a symbol that both articulates the experience of grace, recalls it and perhaps replicates it).

The local community, then, is at least potentially sacramental, particularly in its quintessential manifestation: the sacred tree, the altar, the temple in older times; the volleyball court in the gym in more recent times. One need not experience grace in local community nor use the local community (or its quintessentialization) as a sacramental symbol for sharing and replicating such experiences. However, it must be remarked that many humans have done so and that the importance of Sacred Space has been acknowledged in most communities in human history.

In Eliade's paradox, the organization of a local community is an act of imposing logos on chaos in order to create cosmos. It is a share in the central creative activity of the deity, a continuation of the endless struggle between cosmos and chaos—a struggle which is never finally won. The ordered lanes of the village, the fences and walls around its perimeter, the tilled field beyond that perimeter are cosmos. The prairies or the jungles beyond are still the realm of chaos. In constructing the village and tilling its fields, the people share in the paradigmatic activity of the deity, particularly in the festival ritualization of such activity (ritualizations which are also often an occasion for the transmission of agricultural and "town planning" skills). The village and the fields around it are sacred because they have been created (in the sense of having been "ordered") in communion with the deity. The Sacred Place (the sacred tree, whatever) in the center of the village is the core of the community because it is precisely there that the link with the cosmos-inducing activity of the deity is most pronounced. It is that place, in other words, where grace is most likely to be experienced.

We are not claiming any biological or innate or genetic propensity to experience local community as sacred. We merely are asserting that statistically such experiences seem to be widespread almost to the point of being universal in the human condition and an understandable response to this human, social, cultural and psychological propensity is to consider the neighborhood or the local community a place worth defending. If something is so important as to merit defense, then it also ought to be sufficiently important to produce an occasional "limit experience"[2] now and then.

Doubtless, we have to clear away all of the misperceptions and misunderstandings about the relationship between the sacred and the profane, the meaning of grace, and indeed the meaning of the sacred to enable those engaged in ministerial behavior to think about the local religious community and its buildings as a sacrament, as a symbol of grace, as a place where one is especially likely to encounter the other. Could the gym with volleyball games be terrifying and fascinating? That calls for too much of a stretch of the imagination. Yet it seems true that for many of the young people at Mary, Seat of Wisdom (as well as for many other contemporary "communal Catholics") their experience in the gym (or its equivalent) turns out to be one of the benign encounters they will have with religion during their lives—a link with their religious heritage and the sort of thing they want for their own children. Not quite revelatory perhaps, but maybe a hint of Revelation.

If our observations on local community in the previous chapter are correct, then the sacramental potential (in the sense we are using it here) of local community and the sacred center of local community is enormous. That we have neglected this potential does not make it less enormous.

Religious Symbols in Local Community Socialization

While the sacramental potential of the Sacred Space aspects of local community is enormous, it is not the only reason local religious community is an important component of local community. In the socialization process that goes on in local community there are implicitly understood symbols that the community uses to impart standards and values and norms to the members of the community. Some of these symbols are specifically religious, but there are many different kinds of symbol sets and some of them interact with religious symbols. Our examination of some of the symbols in local community socialization indicates the need for discussions within local communities about the use of symbolic language in the context of specific local communities.

The symbol which is perhaps the most important, and at the same time the least understood, is the symbol of God within the community. What is the community's conception of God? Who do they think God is? Is there any kind of self-conscious definition of God which is operating within the community? The answers to these questions reveal a range of the ways in which the concept of God operates within the local community. One of the easiest dichotomies to use is the continuum between judge and lover, and the question then becomes where does the community place God on that continuum. Children become socialized by hearing and observing various ways in which God is spoken of in the community, but more importantly through the informal personal structures of their lives in which God is mentioned.

Another symbol which is used within the community to socialize individuals is the definition of what a good person is according to community standards. We could make a rough continuum between people who are successful externally and people who are successful internally and test for symbolic differences between communities which lie along the continuum. Some communities judge their members as to whether or not they are good people according to external standards of success such as income, status, property, etc., while other communities tend to judge more according to internal qualities such as the kind of person that one is. (This gets rather confusing since, undoubtedly, social status and property are used as surrogates for internal qualities in many cases, but the theoretical distinction seems valid.)

The same kind of symbolic language that is used about individuals as to whether they are good or not, is also used about the family unit within the community. There are subtle definitions for what a good family is and they may well operate along the internal-external continuum.

Whole family units are therefore socialized by community standards into internalizing a set of values about what it is to be a good family within this community. For example, it is probable that some communities are more child-centered than others and activities and resources devoted to children are weighted more heavily in the judgment of a good family than in other communities which are perhaps more adult-centered. One analogous way to look at this entire process of community socialization is to assume that families socialize individuals and communities socialize families.

One of the more subtle aspects of local community socialization has to do with the symbolic religious value placed on the stages of the life cycle. Some communities are much more conscious of the life cycle processes than others, possibly because they are themselves more heterogeneous with regard to life cycle experiences. Therefore, in communities where you have a mix of both young and old, you are likely to find more awareness of the life cycle and a greater infusion of the life cycle with religious meaning. In communities that are very homogeneous and everyone is the same age it is very difficult to build any kind of symbol around life cycle simply because people are not experiencing it.

Another area where religious symbols seem to be created has to do with the relationships between members of the community and those outside the community. Again, one possibility is that the continuum could run from judging to loving and that some communities are more likely to define outsiders as people to be judged as to their worth while other communities are more likely to define outsiders as people to whom one should be hospitable. The continuum may also run between avoidance and hospitality, which is simply another way of saying judging and loving. It is hard to believe that a community that practiced hospitality to strangers would not leave a mark upon the children and the adults within that community as to the nature of their own social reality. Such hospitable behavior could be easily translated by the individual into a definition of a benign meaning system and other quasi-religious sensibilities.

Still another neighborhood activity which could take on a religious symbol would be that of neighboring. Neighboring is related to hospitality except that it is directed toward those who live in close proximity to the individual as opposed to strangers. This activity could be considered along at least two dimensions: the first, its existence or non-existence within the community; the second, the quality of the neighboring which might range from discussing external matters such as local news and local events to discussing internal matters such as family problems and personal difficulties.

The religious nature of the socialization symbols which are used in the local communities is an important part of the discussion because only religion has a certain kind of socializing power. The analogy we would like to make, while realizing that it limps quite a bit, is with the current discussion of the church in Poland where we have seen that the connection between Polish Catholicism and Polish Nationalism has provided a strong, stable socialization pattern within a given county. In an analogous way the connection between coming from a specific local community and one's own religious identity can provide a strong socialization pattern for future values.

Though there is not yet sufficient empirical data to offer these contributions to the discussion about the use of symbolic language in the local community as more than hypotheses, it does seem that there is an analogous operation within the community that reflects the operation within the family regarding socialization into a set of values. Just as the family provides a socialization context for individual members, so the community provides a socialization context for individual families.

It would also follow theoretically that, just as within the family the most important socializing factor is the relationship between the parents and the attitudes of the father, at least for religious socialization, so, too, the most important factor in the community socialization is likely to be the relationships between families and particularly between the males of those families. For example, regarding the imparting of community values it is probably more important that children see healthy adult relationships between their parents and other significant adults in the community than that they hear positive remarks about the community just from their parents. In some fashion, what we are hypothesizing is that children are raised by a community, not just by their parents. They will get a specific set of messages by observing how their parents interact with others within the community that they cannot get just within the family context. Those messages are critically important for this whole topic of socialization within the local community. Therefore, one of the major factors becomes the friendship networks which the parents themselves engage in. Children need to know how the parents feel about their adult friends, how they interact with them, what they talk about and whether or not that is important.

Thus it becomes clear that both the tendency of people to impute Sacred Space status to their local communities as well as many of the symbols that are used within the community to socialize individuals challenge us to recognize the religious dimension of local community and the need for a religious leadership that will assist people in the process of recognizing that dimension of their lives.

The Process of Religious Encounter

If everything is sacramental with a small s and if humans tend to impute Sacred Space status to their local communities as well as use religious symbols in the process of socializing individuals within these communities, it would seem that within the local community there are many opportunities for encounters with mystery. What we wish to do is suggest an outline of the process of religious encounter and at various points in the outline identify implications for the local church.

The process of religious encounter can be mapped with the metaphors of meeting, understanding and enacting. A person must meet Divine Reality, understand his or her relationship to Divine Reality and, finally, enact the demands of that Reality in concrete personal and social living. At each stage of this process the local church has an important role to play. It provides the environments where a person may become aware of the ultimate Mystery within which they live. It is the place where the tradition and wisdom about this relationship to Mystery is stored and communicated and, finally, it provides opportunities for people to live out this basic faith. We will consider each of these steps.

The first stage in the process of religious encounter focuses on those times and situations where the person becomes aware of an ultimate relationship. This is an emphasis on the times of personal appropriation of inherited religious beliefs. A child may be told that there is a God, that this God loves him or her and that he has certain obligations in relationship to this God. The moment when that knowledge, or that communication, transfers from the realm of something given by the parents to the realm of something personally made aware of is the moment of meeting in the relationship with God. This emphasis on personal awareness is stressed today because secularism, as a structure of consciousness, tends to eliminate it. The secularist consciousness flattens human perception. It allows for all of the discrete and concrete objects of human life to be considered, but it screens out the human relationship to the ultimate Mystery of life itself. Ultimate questions do not get the attention that they deserve because the ultimate relationship to Mystery is not in the forefront of consciousness. At best it is in a fringe position and, therefore, easily set aside.

Another way of saying this is that personal religious experience is at the heart of local church. Oftentimes, when a religion becomes highly structured and organized, as the Catholic religion has, it tends to codify even its religious experiences. It tends to take them for granted and so presuppose them in its theology and worship rather than explicitly focus on them. When it does this there results a mild, rather than enthusiastic religion, a controllable rather than an erratic populus, and an obeyed rather than an inspiring religion. But the cost of this is that personal inspiration and personal contact with Divine Reality is downplayed, and the sources of renewal often dry up.

There are ways of encountering Divine Reality. For our purposes we will consider three paths; the mystical, the mediated and the reflective. These three modes of encounter are on an intensity continuum. The mystical experience is the most intense. It is talked about as an experi-

74

ence of union with God with high feelings of peace, happiness, joy, permeation by the ultimate principle of human life. The mediated experience is less intense. It focuses explicitly on the finite object or situation which caused the person to become aware of the ultimate relationship to God. It does not suggest communion so much as address by God. That you are in the presence of Divine Reality, not that you are in intimate and almost unbearable union with it. The third experience is the reflective, and this is the least intense. There is more mental activity in this experience than the other two. The degrees of suddenness of the other two, the mystical and the mediated, tend to occur to people, they happen to people; the reflective experience is much more directed by the human subject. The person meditates or contemplates, begins the process of human appreciation of themselves and the world they find themselves in, and there comes a point in the mental process when roles seem to be reversed and the person is caught in wonder and awe; the magnitude of the reality they participate in overwhelms their minds and they become aware of a relationship to a larger and infinitely gracious Mystery.

In the past, the local Catholic community facilitated these experiences of Mystery by an emphasis on the church building itself and, within the church, the real presence of Christ in the Eucharist. Although there was never a complete split between the sacred and profane, between the world outside the church building and the world within it, most Catholics understood that there was direct and immediate access to God once they walked through the doors. They blessed themselves with holy water, women put on hats, men took them off, all to signify that they were in the presence of the Sacred. Within the church one could have a reflective experience of God. Many people would sit, and think, and meditate, and consult all there is about who they are. The Eucharist itself was, for many people, a mediated experience of Divine Reality. In and through the host Christ came into a person's heart. Oftentimes, there was a suddenness to the relevation of God's love through this Eucharistic feeding. The building was doubtlessly also the locale for many mystical experiences, times when people seemed to be taken outside of themselves though reports of these are few and far between.

The greater emphasis today is on the presence of God to everyday life. The focus is not so much God's availability in the sacred precincts, but God's accessibility in kitchens and bedrooms, living rooms and streets. The always and everywhere presence of God is more stressed than his specific presence within the Eucharist or within the church building. Greater accessability of God also means a less intense experience. One of the current challenges of local Catholic parishes is to combine a sense of sacred space with the sense of the sacrality of every space, a sense of sacred time along with the sense of a sacrality of every time. This is a difficult task and one that demands great sensitivity.

A story will bring out the differing focuses and also the need for sensitivity. In a worship center on Sunday morning after the liturgies, the people gather in the back for coffee and donuts. It is a large suburban church with a mainly liberal population. And, as the majority of people gather in the back for coffee and donuts, if one is tall one can look over the heads of these people to the front of the worship center where a small group of people are gathered around the tabernacle, kneeling and praying the rosary, or just praying in general. In this small vignette the problem is crystallized. The people in the back have switched the locale of the sacred from the Eucharist itself into their own lives. God is present among them and so they celebrate that Presence both as a faith community in the liturgical activity itself, and then afterward by sharing more fellowship with one another. For some few people within this parish, sacred is still in the host and all the concentration is there, for it is there that God is present and there that God will mediate himself to them. The difference between what could be characterized as a faith community that comes together to express their faith and a religious sensitivity to the awe-inspiring presence of the sacred in the host are two different styles and dictate two different ways of liturgy. The task is not to pit one against the other, but to find ways of integration.

Therefore, the traditional way the local church facilitated religious experiences through a liturgy which emphasized the mystery of human life is now complimented by a different theology that tends to say that the local church emphasizes the presence of God in everyday life as well as in its liturgical services. Therefore, there is a widening of possibilities for people to meet Divine Reality.

There has often been in the past a skepticism with regard to religious experience. It has been argued that certainly some special people have religious experiences— people such as John of the Cross, Teresa of Avilla, Mary Alacoque, but these are exceptions. The vast majority of the people must believe on the word of another. God is notoriously undemocratic; he appears to some, but leaves the majority of the human race in darkness. Therefore, the only hope for the masses is that they believe the revelation of the prophets. This position is backed up by the standard notion of faith that it is believing what it is not seeing.

Although many of the complex convictions of the Christian Catholic faith tradition have come through special revelations to special people, there is a way in which the ordinary person can at least establish the relationship to God. All that goes on within the relationship of special people to God can be appropriated. Circumstances and situations may differ but the relationship itself can be appropriated. This is the distinction William James makes between beliefs and overbeliefs. Overbeliefs are those understandings that come from an explicit faith tradition, but belief itself, the fact that the human person is related to a larger reality and that this larger reality supports and challenges its existence, this fundamental fact can be appropriated by everyone, not only on the authority of another but through their own experiences.

Therefore, the first stage of the process of religious encounter is a meeting with Divine Reality, an understanding that we are related to an Ultimate Reality, and that this relationship is of supreme importance. The local church has a role to play in the facilitation of this meeting. It knows this God and it introduces each person within its community to this God. This process of introduction occurs initially at the Baptism of a child into the community, occurs through the development process in First Communion, and, finally, in its religious education program, finishes the introduction. But there must be more than a meeting, more than an introduction, and this brings us to the second stage in the process of religious encounter.

The second stage of the process of religious encounter is exploring the relationship which was discovered in the first stage. Since the relationship that was discovered in the first stage is an ultimate relationship, it affects all relationships within it. Therefore, if ultimately the human person is related to a gracious and caring Mystery, this relationship has resonances in interpersonal, social and ecological life. In other words, if we construct an ultimate relationship, it influences all proximate relationships. Therefore, the construction of a religious identity has ramifications for all the situations, events and relationships of a person's life. This is the basic meaningfulness of all religious reality: that once the final world is constructed, all the proximate worlds are influenced.

Also, it is at this moment perhaps even more strongly than in the first stage of the process of religious encounter that the persons are aware that they belong to a tradition. Men and women have come before this present generation, have encountered this ultimate relationship, and have spoken in image, story, concept and action about this relationship. We are the inheritors of their wisdom. Although we meet God individually, we do not explore God only individually. We tap into a common tradition that constructs the meaning and truth of our relationship with God and asks us to participate in that relationship through this meaning and truth which our ancestors have discovered and articulated.

This is the enduring and difficult relationship of the individual to a particular tradition. Dangers abound. There are pitfalls everywhere. On one hand, the individual without the tradition is a lost person. We cannot possibly in any one given life explore the relationship to God fully. Life is too short and the giftedness of each life is not as extensive as the giftedness of all of our lives together. Individuals without the tradition feel alienated, alone, on their own, incapable of full understanding and participation. On the other hand, when the tradition becomes overbearing, the individual relationship is lost. The wisdom of the past is no longer a guideline for contemporary experiences and decisions, but it now preempts experience and decision. It brings already determined forms to the present and does not allow creativity or imagination. The past becomes a burden and not a direction. This is an enduring dilemma not only of religious traditions but of all traditions. The question is not to eliminate one of the poles—either individual appropriation or traditional wisdom—the question is to inhabit them creatively so that the well being of the individual and the community are always in the forefront.

An example of how individual experience and traditional wisdom interact can be taken from a workshop that is often done on the parish level. The first procedure of the workshop is to ask the participants to retrieve some time in their lives when they were aware that they were related to a larger reality, to a more, to a whole. They are then asked to share this time with another person in the group. In this sharing they are asked to be very concrete, to refrain from interpretation as much as possible, and to retrieve the experience in terms of its sights, smells and sounds. Once this process is done—a retrieval and a sharing of the experience—the group comes back together and they are asked to name what they felt at the time of this experience. These feelings are put on a blackboard so that the entire group can see them. Although this workshop has been done many times in many different places, the feelings that appear on the board always remain the same. They move from joy to terror, from peace to uncertainty, confidence to vacillation. In other words, human contact with the Ultimate Mystery is an ambiguous affair; it both reinforces and tears down some human expectations.

Once these individual feelings are garnered they are then related to the traditional wisdom. One construction of the feelings that people in the Christian tradition have had when they have encountered God is that they have felt known and loved on the one hand, and judged and called on the other. The individual feelings of the group are then placed within this grid; the experience of being known picks up some of the feelings of the group, the experience of being loved picks up others, the experience of being called picks up others and the experience of being judged picks up others. But for a full understanding of the relationship to the Mystery that they have encountered they need to understand that the Mystery knows and loves, judges and calls. In this way the tradition brings a fuller wisdom about the relationship than is discovered and known partially by each individual. When this occurs the tradition enriches and directs but does not smother or deny the individual's experience.

The role of the local church in this stage of the religious encounter is to make available to people the wisdom of the tradition in a creative non-stifling way. This can be done through homilies, through religious education programs (especially adult religious education programs), through various paraliturgical activities, through discussion groups, etc. But the major question is the availability of Christian wisdom on the relationship to God and therefore on all other relationships we have. How does the Christian tradition get carried into the lives of the latest generation of Christians? It is one thing to talk about a rich tradition, and certainly a religion that has been around for two thousand years has a variety of expressions and certainly a richness of understanding. The question is how available is it. It is one thing to have a rich tradition, it is another thing to be able to mine it and to be in contact with it.

The local church must be the mediating factor, and in particular within the local church the established ministers have to have a knowledge of the tradition in order to be able to bring it forward into contemporary life in a creative and illuminating way. This process has been called befriending the tradition. How do we find the tradition as a friend to the religious dynamics of life? Pastoral leadership must not only be sensitive to the present needs and situations of the community, it must understand the needs and situations of past generations of Christians and their creative responses. We are not the first and, knowing that, we can garner and use the wisdom of those who came before us.

The third stage of the process of religious encounter is the enacting of the meanings we have discovered in the second stage into concrete personal and social life. In the past, the local parish often focused exclusively on this moment of the religious process. It emphasized over and over again the need for moral living, for correct behavior and for the fulfillment of obligations that flow from the first two moments of the encounter. In other words, the logic of belief was stressed over and over again. But it cannot be said too strongly that the logic of belief only makes sense to individuals when they have first encountered the object of belief, God, and have been persuasively convinced of the qualities of that relationship that are elaborated in the second stage. When religion degenerates into morality or moves immediately into the third stage of the process, we have the beginnings of legalism and moralism.

This stage of the religious process is the most complex and calls for the most creative ingenuity. In perhaps an oversimplification, in the first stage of the process, divine initiative is at work and we are in a situation of human response. In the second stage of the process, divine initiative is still at work and human response is corresponding to it, constructing meaning. In this third stage, divine initiative coincides with human initiative. Here we are asked to work out the cause of God in the human situation.

PARISH, PRIEST & PEOPLE

As we emphasized, the relationship to an Ultimate Mystery influences all within that mystery, but the way of influence is not simple. Ultimate convictions and values have to be mediated into concrete situations through thinking and through action. It is one thing to say God is love and therefore we must be loving. It is quite another thing to know how to love, to know what the loving thing is to do in family life, in community life, in political life. The ways of love are infinitely complex. The person who believes in an Ultimate Love will try to master the way of love, try to put his or her energy at the service of love, but this is a complex process and one that is a process of try-and-evaluate, try-and-evaluate.

Yet if this effort is not made—the effort to make concrete the relationship to God, to enact it in human life—we are caught in a type of disintegration or, worse, hypocrisy. We proclaim an ultimate love and an ultimate courage, and yet we do not in any way allow that to influence our behaviors. We are caught under the strictures of John's Gospel that we love God, and we hate our neighbor and, therefore, in John's harsh evaluation, we lie, or in his even harsher evaluation in the Epistles, we turn God into a liar. It seems that the strongest condemnations of the Bible are reserved for those who proclaim a faith in God and yet in no way allow that faith to become flesh in their lives.

The local church has a direct relationship to this stage of the religious process also. It seems to us that in the development of Catholic, local community life, the local church must emphasize the complexities of the process of moral behavior and the pluralistic ways in which they can be embodied. Monolithic understandings of morality will help no one. In other words, the process of moral decision-making must be emphasized and the difficulty of proportionate value-theory and fundamental option must be thoroughly understood. That is, a religious individual come of age must not only understand the religious experience he has had, understand his relationship to the tradition, but also understand the complex ways of making concrete his faith convictions and values.

Besides this, the local church must provide opportunities to grow, opportunities to allow people to escape the traps they often find themselves in, must create a community of care and structure within that community of care situations where people can express love, compassion and understanding. In other words, the local church must be a light on a mountain and salt for the world. It must exhibit in its own life the type of genuine moral concerns that belief in God suggests. These opportunities may vary from concern for other parishes, the raising of money for other places in the world, to a structure of care for those who are sick and elderly in the parish. It may take many different forms but its overall concern is for a community of justice and care and compassion, and it must engender and make possible that community.

When talking about the local community we often rely heavily on psychological and sociological data. Also, we often talk about a faith community and what that means and the historical implications of a faith community. What is often overlooked is that Christianity is a religion. It is built on the foundational dynamics of religious living. Its vitality flows from those dynamics and the fact of its mass appeal is attributable to those mass dynamics. The parish offers a unique dimension to a local community; it is the place that facilitates religious encounter.

The process of religious encounter and enrichment of the tradition requires a "grass-roots" religious community, a sacred place within the community that serves to identify the religious symbols that are present in the socialization process at work in that community. In this place the opportunity to explore the personal imaging in people's lives allows the inherited images to touch upon the life-giving experiences of people. Here theological talk that deals with the enacting of religious encounter can be united with the meeting and exploring level of the encounter.

At Mary, Seat of Wisdom retreat weekends, the death and resurrection theme of the Christian tradition comes alive when it is united with personal stories of death to old ways and resurrection to a new life in the experience of the people. Without a religious community to unite the personal story with the communal story, some of the insights and implications of the commitment to a new life could be ignored. The presence of God in these experiences of mystery could go unnoticed. Garden clubs are all well and good, but they are not in business to bring logos to the chaos of human existence or to help us have a sacred life. They do not offer a sense of hopefulness to those of us who face the challenges of a death-experience, whether that be the physical death of a loved one or the death to self we must undergo at various times in our life cycle. This is the task of the local religious community that has its roots in both the tradition of a community of followers of Jesus and in the experience of people being socialized within their local community.

Before considering more specifically the pastoral mission of the local religious community, we must examine the theological dimension of the concept of local community from the perspective of systematic theology.

CHAPTER 4

Systematic Theology
of the Local Community

OUR bias toward local church began in the experiential and was reinforced by sociological analysis. St. Angela and Mary, Seat of Wisdom are not only good experiences for the people involved; they are also legitimate responses to the human need to belong and to experience the process of socialization. Since this socialization process raises "religious" questions, it would seem to demand a religious community to assist in responding to the questions. We are now faced with the question of whether this local religious community can also legitimately claim to be the "church" for those who participate in it. What basis do we find in the Catholic Christian tradition for claiming that within the local community God is manifested in such a way that the people who experience this manifestation might claim to be the "people of God." Experiential and sociological analysis leads us to theological reflection.

Our realization of the significance of the "local" in human experience causes us to search the Catholic religious and theological tradition for those expressions of Catholic Christianity that render a sense of the concrete *as particular, local*—the *really concrete*—into a natural sense. Catholics, it seems, know as a second instinct that you read the concrete whole—the universal—*only* in and through the journey into your own particularity—*this* family, *this* people, *this* locality, *this* local church, community, folk, heritage.

Catholics know this best when they reflect upon the two classical expressions of Catholic Christianity (every classic in a culture is highly particular in origin and expression yet universal in effect):[1] The first, the religious phenomenon of manifestation; the second, the theological phenomenon of manifestation. Both inform the Catholic lived sense of the reality and central importance of the local church. We will examine both the phenomenon of manifestation and the phenomenon of analogy from the perspective of systematic theology.

The Catholic Religious Classic: Manifestation

There is no one route of Christian manifestation in our period. Indeed it seems that earlier forms of manifestation (the sheer eruption of the power of the cosmos) seem in our day relatively muted. This is true even for those whose religious experience is likely to move in the direction of vision, image, ritual, reflection and mediation. What we find instead are varioius expressions of Christian manifestation alive in our time, with as many distinct journeys as there are foci.

The sheer immediacy of the power of manifestation once overwhelming in our and other cultures is now all too rare. (The eruptions of Mt. St. Helens in 1980 were certainly demonstrations of some power at work, but the diagram of the process at work inside the volcano "explained" the phenomenon; we did not think it the work of the angry gods). Instead we find many routes for the mediation of that immediacy. This "mediated immediacy" *is* present in our cultures and in our parishes. In an age where the sheer immediacy of what Ricouer calls "first naivete" seems spent, and where there are different foci for the different journeys of mediation, the *forms* of mediation become crucial for all.

The most familiar form of mediation in contemporary Catholic theologies remains philosophical. For many theologians, however, and for most "ordinary" Catholics it is the ordinary itself in its real concreteness that is *the* major locus of a manifestation-event. Indeed, the ordinary, once really lived, really embraced and loved, manifests itself *as the extraordinary* revelation of our primordial belonging. Those theologians who have mastered the retrieval of the extraordinaries of the ordinary, free us all to re-experience the ordinary world of body, history, community, nature in all its shocking extraordinariness. Their major point of departure remains, with Bishop Butler and Scotus, the insistence that "everything is what it is and not another thing." Their major discovery—or rediscovery from the mists of childhood memories—is the experience classically expressed by Gerard Manley Hopkins of "the dearest freshness deep down things." They know, with Heidegger, the disclosure of the dignity and common humanity of the world of the everyday manifested in van Gogh's painting of a peasant's shoes. They know, with Gabriel Marcel, the reality of real community in this people, this tradition, this world. They know how extraordinary "ordinary" people really are: their dignity, their uncommon common sense, their tolerance for the weakness of others, their compassion, their *caritas,* their unquestioned sense of belonging to a people. They have not ceased to experience the surprise in every particular. By their taste for the concrete, they possess an astonishing ability to bypass the usual narcissisms and recognize the shocking, lovable, real otherness of the other as particular.

Their rootedness in a family, a people, a community, a tradition, a history frees them to develop systematic pastoral theologies disclosive of reality of the local, the extraordinariness of the ordinary. That same uncrushed sense of surprise and wonder frees them to a real *sense* of this world. Their theologies do not bring in the doctrines of creation and incarnation as afterthoughts. Rather they sense creation—of the body, of sexuality, of community, of nature—as gracious gift to be enjoyed and used in a natural, embodied, sensate, concretely aesthetic way.

In their best exponents, precisely the sense first experienced as a passion for the astonishing concreteness of the particular releases their affectivity and reason to the concreteness of the whole. Simone Weil's profound sense of rootedness in her people freed her to be alive to the sufferings and the dignity of a global humanity. Those whose actual involvement in ecology is grounded in this real sense of the world in its astonishing concreteness enter the ecological movement because, unlike most of their fellow Christians and Jews, they need not retreat when they hear Eliade's pointed question to us all: "Do modern Christians and Jews any longer really *feel* the world as God's creation? Do Christians really believe the reality of incarnation?" The illuminative and participation motifs of Eastern Christianity, the patristic vision of the goodness of existence, the radical immanence of God in all nature, the sensed reality of *each* human being as the "imago dei"—all these traditional and half-forgotten symbols of the tradition take new life in those theologies of manifestation.

They refuse to restrict the true scope of God's grace to

the forgiveness of our troubled, introspective, "isolate," Western Consciences. Rather, like the whole Eastern Christian tradition, like Bonaventure, Hopkins, Wordsworth and the Romantics in the West, they retain and develop this healing sense for the concrete. They embark upon a journey of intensification into the concreteness of each particular reality—*this* body, *this* people, *this* community, *this* tradition, *this* family, *this* place, *this* moment, *this* other—until the very concreteness of any particularity releases them to the concreteness of the whole.

For some, however, the emphasis falls elsewhere: not on the ordinary but on the extraordinary as the clue to reality. One of the surest clues to this second route of manifestation is Mircea Eliade's revealing comment: "only the paradigmatic is the real." (For him, the paradigmatic is *out of* ordinary time and space and thereby liberates one to the "really real" world of sacred time and sacred space.) Indeed, Eliade's own great works, from his scholarly breakthrough in "the dialectic of the sacred and the profane," to his brilliant novel *The Forbidden Forest* vibrates with this disclosive sense of the paradigmatic, the extraordinary experience.

From the privileged moments releasing "involuntary" memories in Proust to the privileged moment of the Eucharist in the parish, one finds in the modern world this other path of manifestation: a path where only the extraordinary—only the *involuntary* memory, only the privileged mountain, tree, rock, place frees us to the power of manifestation.

In every human life there are certain privileged places, times, events, rituals, images, persons which each of us recognizes as the disclosure of *truth* by which I really live. In Catholic life the same kind of sense for the privileged and the extraordinary occurs. The liturgical year for the sacramental Christian can become the occasion to free the self from the reality of an overwhelming profaneness into the pulsating and liberating rhythms of the extraordinary founding events of Jewish and Christian history (Exodus, exile, nativity, epiphany, advent and lent, Good Friday, Easter and Pentecost) as these events live in celebration in both tension and harmony with the external rhythms and moods of the seasons.

From the shock of truth in a real liturgical life in a parish to the great icons of the East, the experience of the freedom allowed by a real refusal to domesticate the extraordinary occurs. Beneath all our necessary suspicion of the sentimentalizing, mythologizing hagiography of the saints lies the power of these lives to disclose their singular truth: the truth of a life lived on the wager that "only the paradigmatic is the real." To read, for example, Edith Sitwell's studies of British eccentrics is to be intrigued and amused by the wondrous possibilities of the human spirit. But to read the great Teresa of Avila or even the "little" Therese of Lisieux is to recognize another possibility for the human spirit: how beyond even their and our obvious neuroses, beyond even their and every society, beyond even the explosive extraordinariness in the passionate character of Theresa and the real ordinariness in Therese lies their common secret: really to live life is to live it as if, "only the paradigmatic is the real."

From the extraordinary experiences in all our lives— today perhaps especially in the experience of sexuality as the last outpost of the extraordinary in many lives—to the classical events, persons, rituals, images and myths scattered as signs of releasement throughout our religious heritage, the shock of recognition in and by the power of the paradigmatic reverberates. That sense lives even in a world that has tried to conquer nature, denied the body, and emptied the mythic unconscious of its healing powers. Yet some still prevail to teach us the truth that even now this journey of manifestation may still be taken. When we recognize the truths disclosed in the writings of Proust, Jung, Eliade, when we recognize that some persons can only be named "saints," when we recognize even in our battered liturgies and our domesticated sacraments their enduring, healing privileged truth, when we find recognizability in the welcome works of fantasy of our period, in the liberating experiences of body, nature, dreams, the erotic, we all lay claim to the truth of this particular journey wherein the intensification of the sense of the extraordinary becomes an event of manifestation of and by the whole. In some matters, "only the paradigmatic is the real."

What especially characterizes both these distinct journeys to the event of manifestation is the importance in each of *some form* of *particular* mediation. Whether the mediating reality be the ordinary in all its myriad forms, or the representative mediation of the extraordinary and the sacramental, the importance of some mediating reality endures. Moreover, the great temptation of all expressions of manifestations—the idolatrous temptation to allow the mediating vehicle to become identified as the power-event of manifestation itself—is *never* countenanced by any authentic expression of mediated manifestation. All the finite, natural, sensate, *particular* mediations of the sacraments represent but do not constitute the sheer event of graced manifestation. Christian icons and saints disclose, never displace *the* paradigmatic manifestation of God and humanity alike for the Christian, the event called Jesus

Christ. In the authentic spirit of manifestation, finally, all reality discloses the all-prevasive power of grace, the radical immanence of God in the epiphanies of nature, through the classical events of Jewish and Christian history to the "inner journey" of each human being, each "imago dei" to the incarnation-manifestation of Jesus Christ, the event of God.

The Catholic Theological Classic: Analogy

A relative constant in the extremely pluralistic reality of Catholic theologies is the presence of analogical language. What might this tell us? For our purposes, it tells us this: like its religious analogue, manifestation, the theological language of analogy discloses the presence of a Catholic analogical imagination (for more background on this topic see David Tracy, *Proceedings of the Catholic Theological Society of America,* 1977). Here we will consider the essential form of analogical language and then develop some of the implications this has for our discussion of the importance of local community.

The form is this: the key to analogical language is the presence of some extraordinary *focal meaning* which allows one to work out—through the efforts of a theological imagination—some set of *ordered* relationships of God, self and world. The focal meaning provides the key to all those relationships. We imagine the world *as if* that focal meaning really were the key to the order of the whole of reality—God, self, world. Suppose that focal meaning is the religious one of manifestation. Suppose the theological word for that manifestation is incarnation—the real incarnation of God in Jesus Christ. *Thereby* there is disclosed the radical immanence of God in all, in the concrete, the particular, the ordinary which is now recognized *as extraordinary.* With that focal meaning one can begin to work out ordered relationships for the whole of reality (God, self, world). What will they look like?

By concentrating attention upon that focal meaning—the event of grace named the Incarnation—Catholic theologians develop their ordered relationships for the whole. This event is the fundamental control because the focal meaning for all those ordered relationships will be present in it (the incarnational event as the self-revelation of God, disclosing the true nature of the human and the world alike). The secondary (but crucial because transformative) controls for articulating those relationships will be the particular focus of the fundamental questions from the basic experience of the human situation (death, transience, sin, alienation, oppression, trust, joy, love, order) along with the forms of critical reason and lived *praxis* employed to understand and articulate those questions critically.

The reality of God, to be sure, is no single focus of a single ordered relationship in any theology worthy of the name. Rather, so, too, in their ways, do our other two primary candidates for ordered relationships: self and world. For every symbol from the originating revelatory event of grace to the final understanding of God encompassed by the entire symbol system, is also, at the same time, an understanding of self and world. Every human understanding of God is at the same time an understanding of oneself—and vice versa. Every proper understanding of the self is never an understanding of some unreal isolated self but of a self in intrinsic internal relationships, in intrinsic coexistence with the reality of the "world." The world is the reality of those other selves, of society, history and the cosmos.

It is, therefore, impossible to separate these realities God-self-world. It remains possible, as Catholic theology has insisted, to distinguish them, to understand them distinctly and on their own terms as far as possible *in order to unite* these mutually reenforcing realities into the ordered relationships of a systematic theology.

For us the overwhelming reality disclosed in the originating event of the grace of Jesus Christ is none other than grace itself. From the first glimmers of that graciousness in the limit-questions of our situation though the wonder disclosed in the event of grace revealed in explicit religious experience to the focused concreteness of that graciousness revealed in the event of Jesus Christ, grace prevails and finally triumphs as the pervasive and transformative clue to all reality. Grace overcomes the otherwise overwhelming sense of the meaningless and absurdity of our existence lost, as Pascal reminds us, "in this remote corner of nature," the frightening spectacle of the massive suffering endured by human beings, indeed by all creation, from the beginning to the demonic outbursts of anti-Spirit (Auschwitz, Hiroshima, and the Gulag) in our own century. We now yield to that other clue, that other faith and story disclosed decisively in the revelation of the graciousness of God, the graced reality of self and world in the event of Jesus Christ. In being thus released, we are not freed to some new knowledge which we now control. Rather we are finally freed to embrace that fundamental trust in the whole which is faith. We are free to demand of ourselves, by that trust, a hope for the sake of the hopeless, to risk the seemingly impossible gospel possibility of living a life of that faith and that hope working through that love given as gift and demand.

The reality disclosed in Jesus Christ undoes at the core any claims to gnosis, any temptations to triumphalism, any false complacency in ourselves as graced or even in God as gracious, any flight into sentimental notions of love untouched by the passion for justice.

Who, in this perspective, is God? God is the power not our own disclosing herself/himself: in philosophy as the *one* strictly necessary individual; in religious experience as the graced reality of the whole by the power of the whole; in the Christian experience of the Christ-event as the power of pure, unbounded love—that ultimate reality which grounds and pervades all reality. As that power of graciousness, God affects all and is affected by all. Love, and love alone, is the surest clue to who God is and thereby to what reality in its ultimate meaning in spite of all else finally is. That reality of gracious love is experienced religiously and understood theologically through its presence-in-union with the event of Jesus Christ. Theologies focused upon manifestations, in understanding God as Love and Grace, will deny any claims to control of that experience or that knowledge. They will deny understandings of the radical incomprehensibility of God on the other side of all *our* best comprehensible schemas of theological intelligibility. They will forge, for and in our actual situation, understandings of the presence of God in God's very absence in the situation. Above all, they will return, again and again, to the radical mystery of who God as Love and Power is to all who have felt that presence.

In that manner, do the manifestation traditions in Catholic theology develop their trusting understandings of the graced, self-transcending self. Eros is transformed but not negated by divine agape; that transformation is *caritas.*

Reason is sublated but never disowned by the faith which seeks understanding: that sublation is theology. The sensate, sexual, aesthetic reality of our embodied selves will be transformed but should not be negated in the spiritualities emerging from that experience of gifted trust. In turn, those transformations become Christian understandings of the created giftedness of body, sexuality, beauty.

Although the emphasis in all such manifestation-focused theological understanding of the self is clearly upon the presence of God's gift of grace to all reality, it is not the case that such emphasis disowns the reality of our present incompleteness. The very sense of *giftedness* in negating all pretensions to self-achievement, in the negations of sin and sins as failures to "hit the mark" and as disorienting to the true meaning of the self, in the negations of all rationalisms foolishly presuming to control or manipulate that gift, in the recognitions of the radical ambiguity of the self, and in the refusal of any easy optimism in the self in favor of long-range optimism also recognizes the not-yet of our present situation.

In the nature-grace typologies so often employed in these theologies to understand the self, *grace* is the category employed to understand our concrete existence. Grace and its sheer giftedness is the reality which allows us to understand the giftedness of nature. The reality of God as love revealed in the event of grace named Jesus Christ is the central clue to the meaning of the self as one loved and loving. In Christian systematics there is no theology which is not also an anthropology. There is no Christian anthropology that is not also a theology. The Christian doctrine of God and of the human rise and fall together. The key to both—and thereby to their interrelationships—may be found in the harsh, demanding reality of radical, agapic love. (For more on this see: David Tracy, *The Catholic Model of Caritas.*)

In understanding the realities of God and self, the theologian is already understanding the reality named world. For the God who affects and is affected by the self affects and is affected by all. God as love affects and is affected by the self as a self-in-world. Self and world are co-existents which can be distinguished but never separated. Both are co-posited by God and thereby affected by that God who is love and who as love is, in turn, affected by self and world.

The particular focus chosen to understand God and the self is, at the same time, the central clue to the aspect of world that is emphasized in a particular theology. Certainly those theologies which have their major focus in the realities of manifestation and incarnation are most alive to certain signal realities in that complex phenomenon named world.

With their profound understanding of radical giftedness and thereby of God's radical, loving immanence in all, these theologies are open to that sense of grace in all reality. Nature and body, not only history and spirit, are felt as graced and thus understood in theologies of creation, incarnation and sacrament. The mutuality present in authentic friendship and real community are recognized as the graced realities they are. The somewhat ordered fragile relationships of justice in society, like the ordered reality of authentic tradition, are honored as the graced, gifted realities they are.

And just this recognition of the all pervasive reality of grace, of the need to focus upon every concrete particular manifestation in the light of the self-manifestation-incarnation of God in Jesus Christ is the religious and theological vision that comes as an impulse to form a "second sense" in Catholics for the local, the concrete, the particular. That "second sense" is what *must be* the second sense alive in real parish life, a sense that, yes, God and God's reality are really here in this particular community. Yes, the paradigmatic which *is* the real is none other than Jesus Christ. And what that clue reveals to us here is the extraordinariness of the ordinary—of the local, the concrete, the particular as our proximate clue here and now to the whole. To miss *that* clue is to risk missing the extraordinary reality present to and in it. It is to miss the fact that the all (God-self-world) is best understood *in and through* the particular. For if God *is* love, if all *is* graced, then the surest route to that love and to that universality is here, now, and in the really concrete, the "each," the local and the particular.

So it is that the Catholic religious and theological traditions with their emphasis on manifestation (incarnation-sacrament-grace) and analogy form our common unquestioned and graced sense that *in* the concrete, the particular, the local lies the paradigmatic clue to the whole. The people of St. Angela and Mary, Seat of Wisdom, responding to the human need to belong to a local, socializing community where they experience religious questions, would expect to find within that community some clues to *the* answer to all their questions. Reflection from the perspective of Catholic systematic theology adds to our convictions concerning the importance of the local parish community.

CHAPTER 5

Pastoral Theology and the Local Church

IF our experimental and sociological analysis and theological reflections up to this point have been correct, we are now in a position to ask: why is it that many local parishes are not providing religious community for their members? If people need to belong to a local community where, through the process of socialization, they experience religious questions, and if we believe that the surest route to the God who *is* love is in the really concrete, the local and the particular, why is it that many Catholics find little in their parish experience to assist them as they confront the religious questions of their daily lives? Why are there so few parishes like Mary, Seat of Wisdom? Why do some Catholics still call for the dismantling of local parish in favor of smaller, more manageable religious communities?

The answer to these questions is two-fold: parishes are not true religious communities when there is ineffective pastoral leadership and they are not religious communities when there is no articulated (or at least commonly held) vision of what a parish is. Both parts of the answer are interrelated. It is impossible to imagine how effective pastoral leadership could long survive in a parish with no vision of what it means to be a parish; it is equally difficult to imagine a parish vision developing in the absence of effective pastoral leadership. Initially, for the purposes of our study of positive pastoral leadership, we need to consider a theological vision of parish based on insights of the previous chapters.

We recognize the importance of local community and the significance of the Catholic traditions of manifestation and analogy. We now turn to pastoral theology for an understanding of how to relate these two insights to the modern phenomenon of local parish. We will not consider a theological vision for a particular parish; rather, we will examine visions that could be adapted to the circumstances of most parishes. We now address ourselves to the issue of theological vision to establish the background for the type of pastoral leadership we will recommend in the remainder of the study.

We cannot begin to consider the leadership qualities needed in the parishes of the eighties without examining the role of theological vision of parish in both the past and the present. In the American experience of neighborhood/parish there was a theological vision that gave rise to the roles played by the various members of the community. Though this vision was seldom articulated, it was based on a common acceptance of the Church as the continuing source of salvation for the individual and the world. The parish as the local unit of the Church was accepted by both clergy and laity as *the* place where salvation was guarded and passed on. One seldom quit going to Church, in the past, because one disagreed with the Pope or local bishop, but many people stayed away from the church after a disagreement with the pastor. The pastor was viewed as the guardian of the faith.

As the parish moved into a post-Vatican II period this

common theological vision faded. Many problems associated with parish leadership come from a lack of agreement on the role of the parish and of parish leadership. Even those parishes that are functioning effectively today face difficulties when they continue to have an unarticulated theological vision. Though the present leadership and the rest of the parish might now be operating out of a shared unarticulated theological vision, there is no guarantee that new pastoral workers and leaders will be attuned to this vision.

Those parishes that have begun to articulate a theological vision realize that the vision functions as a servant and facilitator of Christian living. It orders the experiences of the individuals and community into meaningful patterns and asks the members of the community to participate in the vision, integrate it into their personalities and live out its symbols. It is not enough for the people of Mary, Seat of Wisdom to hear homilies on the meaning of the kingdom of God (though they should hear many such homilies); they must be able to relate their role as participants in the kingdom to their personal experiences and they must want to pass the message of the kingdom on to the next generation. They are more apt to be able to do this when there is an articulated vision of the parish as the continuing representative of Christ's message about the kingdom of God.

The theological vision will be able to spark a response from the people of the community when it emerges from the interaction of the experience of the community and the beliefs of the religious tradition, shapes itself around the problems, confronts current problems, and gives creative expression to the spirit of the age. This understanding of the experience of the community must then be able to prosecute the inherited tradition, asking specific and pointed questions of the fund of human wisdom found in the Christian tradition. People in Mary, Seat of Wisdom experiencing the questions of socialization at various stages of the life cycle must be able to ask how this relates to their membership in a community continuing the message of the kingdom of God. What insights does that message have for the marital problems they experience during a mid-life crisis? Hopefully, in the dialectical relationship between their present situation and the wisdom of the tradition (perhaps the insight of "dying to the old in order to rise to new life"), a direction for a usable future takes shape. An effective theological vision is one that rallies revelation and tradition around present problems in such a way that future possibilities are opened up.

And it is the need for new possibilities—for the ability to hope that things can be different, that the chaos of the present situation can somehow be integrated into an ongoing experience—that highlights another important function of theological vision. Theological vision would not merely inform people at Mary, Seat of Wisdom that they belong to a community that believes it is continuing the work of Jesus as messenger of the Kingdom of God. It would also situate the person, and the whole community, in a certain relational character vis-a-vis existence. The vision of messenger of the kingdom of God would give a direction to life—mark out a path that challenges the couple in a marital crisis to seek whatever information they need to solve the crisis—but it also would offer them the assurance that God's agapic love is available to transform their *eros* and allow them to begin to mend their relationship. It would inspire them to make necessary adjustments. It would empower them when they lack the strength to overcome seemingly impossible obstacles.

In summary, we would say that theological vision emerges from the dialogue between contemporary experience and religious tradition, shaping itself around the problems of the culture. While it functions as a servant and facilitator of Christian living it also orients us toward the future and gives direction to the innumerable and undifferentiated experiences of our lives. All religious communities are guided by some theological vision, though, for the most part, it continues to remain unarticulated. So often the vision the pastor is using when he determines his leadership role is quite different than the one adhered to by the parishioners. He might still be guided by the vision of the local parish as the guardian of the faith, while his people have begun to think of themselves as members of the People of God. Conversations about the future of the parish never get off the ground because the participants to the discussion are talking past each other. An important task for every parish is the structuring of a theological vision for the particular parish with its own experiences and its relationship with the Catholic Christian tradition.

The actual task of structuring a vision is an exercise in theologizing from experience, in allowing the theological imagination to order and orient. Within the Catholic community this structuring of a vision, as well as its proclamation, contributes much to the contemporary understanding of the role of priest and pastoral leadership. We have attempted to structure two such visions based on two different approaches to contemporary experience. Neither of these visions are offered as specific visions to be adopted by a parish, but both of them grow out of theologizing from experiences in contemporary parishes. Both recognize the importance of local community and both demand pastoral leadership that will encourage the community to respond to the challenge of the vision.

Middle America (West or South Side Chicago)

If, as Carl Rogers once claimed, the problem of tomorrow (which is probably already today) will be the ability to absorb change, it is important that a theological vision stress both permanence and change in the Catholic community. The vision of the parish as a historical people helps creatively explain and answer this problem.

The image of the parish as a historical people calls forth Paul's image of the People of God. The emphasis on history is an emphasis on the radical implications of what it means to be in space and time and a radical reluctance to escape into a spiritual or eschatological church. This image relates directly to the problem of continuity and discontinuity and of maintaining identity in change. In its history, the Church has adapted to new environments: the hellenization of the early Palestinian church, the Constantinian alliance, the adopton of feudal systems.

Part of the disillusionment with Church today is due to the a-cultural rendering of tradition. Ideally, the Church, having the longest memory of any existing institution and a heritage of reformation to call upon, should be suited to understand and explain change. The image of parish as a historical people provides a model not only to assimilate change but also to direct and initiate it. The same image also reflects a connective sense of history and provides a basis for understanding permanence and continuity.

In addition, the image of the parish as a historical people might also help meet the crisis of rootlessness. Even though we build communities wherever we go, the ones we build today often seem to lack the traditional stability and direction of the older ethnic groupings. In the framework of a larger, non-nationalistic people (parish) the sense of purpose and direction so persistently sought might have a chance of being found. A historical people vicariously extends a person's background, gives her a value tradition to draw on (or reject), and grounds her in a reality larger than she is. An historical person now has inherited and belongs to the spirit of the people who came before her. This spirit of struggle and hope, originally bequeathed by Jesus, adheres in the historical order by means of structure and statement but is always more than these. Membership in this people serves as a potential source of identity and strength. So the local church, taking the lead from the contemporary crisis of change and rootlessness, might begin to image and promote itself as a historical people.

But this does not say enough, for it does not mention the task of this historical people. A more complete model of the local church would be: *an historical people who continue the work of Jesus at this time and in this place.* This addition might not seem to clarify and direct a people but to embroil them in endless christological controversies. What the exact work of Jesus was can be endlessly argued but the idea of double sacramentality employed by Schillebeeckx serves the situation well. Jesus revealed humankind in our true relationship to God and God in his true relationship to us. This revelation of man and God is still the task of the Church, the continuation of Christ, at this time and in this place.

What does it mean to reveal humankind and reveal God? First, let us consider what it might mean *to reveal us.* There is the problem of a "knowledge gap" in our

106

modern society. As Peter Drucker maintains, knowledge, or rather the skill based on knowledge, might well become the cutting edge of society. There are, in our society, those who have knowledge and those who do not have it. In our nation the line of demarcation in the future might well be not between black and white or even rich or poor, but between the knowledged and unknowledged.

In our society the local Roman Catholic Church is in an advantageous position to bridge the knowledge gap. The majority of "church-going" people are from the working middle-class. It is this class, even more than the poor, who feel alienated from knowledge. This estrangement from the knowledge culture turns either to inferiority or hostility toward the "egghead world." But the Church is also at home in the exploding world of knowledge. It has a vested interest in education and trains its personnel in the sciences of humans and community. Could not the Church mediate between these two segments of our society? The need is blatant—specifically in interpersonal and inter-communal fields; in the insights of biology, theology, sociology, philosophy, medicine, and psychology, in the areas of the "emotional and spiritual life of man." Could not the local Church partially function as "journeyman" and "the knowledge base" for our future growth? The knowledge of humankind and our environment has a pastoral dimension. Knowledge may not be virtue but it can heal and enlighten and free. It delights and puzzles and reveals the wonders and complexities of humankind for this time and in this place and so continues the work of Jesus.

"Revelation is revolution in religious knowledge." But since the enlightenment the standard approach of official religion to knowledge has been either to ignore it or to push faith into a transcendental realm where the stumbling human mind could not pursue. The rise of the physical and social sciences was seen to radically challenge the validity of religious knowledge. The acids of biology, sociology, and psychology, so the argument ran, threatened to dissolve the distinctiveness of religious experience. But it seems in many ways just the opposite has occurred. The knowledge explosion in secular fields has spurred renewed attention to the field of religious phenomena, not to arbitrarily debunk but to explore and understand with more sensitive methods of discernment. Because of the underlying unity of the human person an increase in knowledge of one dimension of man's multiplex existence precipitates study of the other dimensions in the light of this new knowledge. All the sciences and arts work together to reveal man in his predicaments and potentialities.

A sound instinct in the American Church has been its close association with education. Perhaps past reasons for this were clanish, designed to "circle the wagons," to help the cognitive minority of immigrant Catholics to survive. Today's reasons however should be outgoing, designed to uncover man and his world. Etymologically, education, to draw out, and revelation, to uncover, seem to suggest a similar process. Perhaps the words could be used to explain each other. "Education" has picked up overtones of arrogance and power; "revelation" might have the more positive connotations of discovery and enlightenment. What this contemporary revelation is about is the richness of life, a life redeemed from the suffocating effects of mere quantity, a life open to the Spirit. Could not the local church move in this area of pastoral knowledge, not as a sideline activity, but as a direct consequence of its theological vision? This would be an effort to respond creatively to its environment and to continue the revelation of humankind at this time and in this place.

To reveal God correlates with this revelation of humankind in the mysterious unity and density of our experience. But this interrelatedness is not an excuse to dissolve one into the other. The Church must know what it is about when it speaks of God. No exaggerations, glib references, or anemic appeals to a refuge faith will be accepted. Within the current cultural shake-up the Church can no longer presuppose a faith in God and build its liturgy and law upon it. Rather it must examine what cultural presuppositions can be used in creating an atmosphere where personal and communal faith becomes possible. This "apologetic orientation" must become the presupposition of the local Church. The problem of the presence and absence of God must be faced and not avoided.

There is something escapist about an exclusive appeal to the past when speaking of God. Most surely Christianity is rooted in history, and it has a tradition of the mighty acts of God in space and time, the mightiest of which is Jesus. But the appeal to the revelation of God in past events is not meant to be an apologetic reassurance because today God is nowhere to be found. Rather it is meant to show God's fidelity to his people—as he was with them in the past, he is with them now, and will be with them in the future. Man today cannot live solely on the community's memory of its paradigmatic events, even when this memory is sacramentally reenforced. For surely one of the characteristics of man is that he forgets. The historical forms of God's presence may act as a guide to discover his presence today but they can in no way substitute for his absence.

Likewise, there is something escapist about an exclusive appeal to the future when speaking of God. Eschatology may well be the focus that will reconfigure our image of God. It seems to be able to provide a horizon for the finest elements in developmental psychology, process philosophy and evolutionary biology and the demand that Christians seek social justice. But the category of eschatology does not exhaust the dimensions of Christian experience. Hope for the future, when God will be all in all, must be rooted in a present experience of God, however dim and incomplete. If it is not, Freud's comment that belief may be an illusion because its motivation is mere wish-fulfillment and not a relation to experienced reality is an accurate description. The once and future God who is not now is an illusion.

The quest and question of God, although supported by the past and looking to the future, has its initial locus in present, personal, human experience. But this experience should not be fluoroscoped for the immediate, direct presence of God or held waiting for a personal theophany. The revelation of God in human experience is indirect.

This idea of an indirect revelation of God is strongly supported by the symbolic character of God-talk. Man does not speak directly of God but rather of the dimension of human experience in which God is encountered. The Unconditioned, the Ultimate, the Given of life reaches man in, through, and under human experience. God is not a separable element of reality nor is God encountered in a single, definable experience. Rather God is encountered in the depth and ultimacy of every experience. The Divine is not another being among beings but Being itself, the power and ground of *all* that is. God lives, so to speak, within the density and ambiguity of human experience and so the divine image is entrapped in space and ravaged by time like all things human. The struggle to bring to speech this God whose presence is felt in the complexities of human interaction is symbolic and indirect. The route from a literal to a symbolic understanding of God is the route the Church must travel.

If the revelation of God happens indirectly in present, human experience, what does it mean that the parish must reveal God? The parish must also pursue its task indirectly, making possible God's self-revelation in contemporary experience by safeguarding the human. The place of the encounter between God and man is the depth of human and interhuman experience. Here the initial glimmer is seen and the question asked that is the prerequisite to faith. But in our society many forces militate against the human. Some would make the human a mind; others a belly. Some would manipulate the human for profit; others program it through an IBM 320. Some would admit to the ranks of the human only what is good; others only what is evil. The human as the central focus out of which life is viewed is in constant danger of usurption by money, achievement, and the greatest threat of all, power. If the Church is to reveal God, it must proclaim and safeguard this human at this time and in this place.

The mission of parish as a historical people who continue the work of Jesus (the revelation of God and us) at this time and in this place is grounded in the problems of change, rootlessness, the knowledge gap, and the threat to the human posed by unbridled technocracy, misguided politics and the paradox of conglomerate yet isolated living. This cultural base makes the "selling of the vision" more a matter of recognizing inherent need than of advertising technique. This vision serves Christian living by explicating a "church-identity," bringing it into increased consciousness, and so reinforcing the commitment of the people and supporting their efforts in the world. This vision also orients, maps out the future, and deploys the energies and skills of the people in specific directions (pastoral knowledge and safeguarding the human).

Suburban America (Any Suburb, USA)

Another way of structuring a theological vision for a parish is to consider the primary focus of the lives of the parishioners and attempt to prosecute the Christian traditions with the concerns that surround that focus. This second vision of parish grows out of reflection on the American situation of the suburban neighborhood/parish and the family. Though it would not apply to all parishes, the experience of family is appropriate as an increasing number of Americans indicate that they hope to gain their greatest sense of satisfaction in life from marriage and the husband-wife, parent-child relationships within the family.

The family is filled with experiences of the mystery of human life. This results from both genetic and cultural factors that have led to the formation of the family unit as a way of regulating the economic contract in which the product is children. Anthropologists claim that very early on in human history emotional bonds must have formed between the members of this economic contract. Once emotional bonds form, we are confronted with concerns about the others, concerns that lead to questions about the meaning of life. Today, with increased life expectancy, those concerns extend over prolonged periods of time and involve people in different sets of relationships with various members of the family over the years. A child grows to adulthood and both he and his parents must learn new ways of relating. As the parent ages and often develops a dependency on the child the relationship takes on new overtones. And each period of family life has its own stresses and concerns, which often overshadow the joys that could be present in familial love.

While family members are undergoing various familial crises, the parish is the place where they are exposed to images and stories of God along with the insights and implications of many of these stories. Considering our earlier outline of the process of religious encounter, we could say that within the familial relationships many people have experiences that could well be experiences of mystery. When parish has been successful for the process of religious encounter of its members it has, often unconsciously, led people to an awareness and acknowledgement of the presence of this mystery, so as to form a link between the experience of the family and the images, stories and insights of the tradition as well as the implications of this for the particular experience.

Putting together these insights about the family and those we have of the neighborhood/parish, as well as those gained from our understanding of the Catholic traditions of manifestations and analogy, it seems possible to propose a theological vision of parish as the place where family members, individually and as a family, have the opportunity to articulate their experience of the mystery of human life and have this articulation verified and accepted or rejected by the larger Christian tradition. Here, too, they receive the support to respond to the mystery of God as revelation in their lives.

In more traditional language we could say that the parish is *the Spirit-filled community which knows of God's*

New Leadership for the Local Church

plan of salvation through Jesus Christ and proclaims this in celebration and fellowship.[1] Reflection on the presence of mystery in familial life makes it clear that a Spirit-filled community is made up of individuals who have innumerable encounters with mystery in their familial relationships. These relationships at times encourage and at other times inhibit the ability of people to respond to the call of Jesus. If the encounter with mystery in the family situation is ignored in the celebration and fellowship the community misses the richness of mystery in its own experience.

This is not an attempt to make a parish a strictly family-centered community. It should not lead to a focusing of all the parish resources on that stage of family life when the children are in school. Indeed such a focus would no longer qualify a parish as family-centered. Now that there is increased recognition of the influence of familial relationships beyond the school age period, this narrow view is no longer possible. Nor should this vision limit the parish to focus only on those experiences of mystery that are familial. We cannot limit grace to one particular form of mediation. However, a parish that is concerned about the experiences of mystery in familial experiences recognizes the importance of familial relationships for all other areas of people's lives. Even those parishioners who are not members of a parent-child family unit or a husband-wife unit, have now, or have had in the past, familial relationships that confront them with the experience of mystery.

The mystery encountered in familial relationships, when understood in light of the Christian tradition, frees an individual to understand the mystery encountered in all relationships. The admonition to settle one's differences with a brother before making an offering to God recognizes the importance of working through the problems of human intimacy in a familial relationship. This is the key for uncovering the presence of God in all of life. Once we discover how the Christian tradition assists us with the process of familial intimacy, we have a better understanding of how to respond in situations beyond the family.

The Christian, who knows how to die to self in a marital relationship in order to allow himself and his spouse to grow in love, is learning how to transform his narcissism in areas other than just his marriage. So, too, a parish which addresses the presence of mystery within familial relationships responds to the primary religious experience of its members and prepares them to be open to the mystery of human life wherever they encounter it. The God discovered when people become adept at the skills of human intimacy is a God who does not disappear when we leave a familial setting. The parish offers its members the opportunity to allow God's grace to transform familial religious experiences. In turn, the parish then becomes a community of grace-filled members who announce this grace beyond the family and parish.

Both of these theological visions recognize that the identity of the parish resides in its theological vision. If the parish is not sure of itself or what it should do, perhaps its theological vision is not focused or how the vision functions is not understood. The theological vision of St. Angela was understood in an unarticulated manner by all those involved in the community. At Mary, Seat of Wisdom, there is a conscious effort to continuously address the need for a theological vision and to refine the significance of that vision for the specific circumstances of the parish. At the present time in Catholic history, a parish without an explicit use of a theological vision dissipates its energies and runs headless into the future. It will not be the place where the reality of God as love is experienced. Manifestation will not be apparent in its midst.

As both of these visions demonstrate, the parish is the mediating agent between the experiences of its members, as people belonging to a local community where the socialization process raises religious questions that require a process of religious encounter if they are to be properly answered, and the Catholic traditions of manifestations and analogy. A parish with a theological vision has a focus for its process of mediation.

We conclude this section on the reasons for our bias toward local parish with a realization that we still must seek an answer to the question of who has the responsibility for leading the process of structuring a theological vision and guiding its articulation. This rather long introduction to our proposal for pastoral leadership in the local church has been necessary to underscore the basis for our bias toward local church as well as to highlight the importance of pastoral leadership to organize the task of focusing the theological vision of parish. Neither St. Angela nor Mary, Seat of Wisdom could be considered "parishes that work" without strong pastoral leadership. The remainder of our study will examine the type of leadership necessary in a parish that seeks to uncover the God who is already present in its midst.

PART TWO

Leadership in the Local Church

CHAPTER 6

Religious Authority

WE begin this portion of our study of pastoral leadership with two stories. The first story concerns an American bishop and his diocese. According to the bishop, "I don't think I have given one order here in the last ten years." Yet his diocese is one of the most efficiently run administrative units in the entire church. This bishop runs both a highly democratic and highly efficient diocese. When this bishop, who was educated at a time when bishops gave orders and clergy and laity followed those orders, was asked why he did not give orders, his reply was, "Because nobody listens to them anymore."

The second story concerns a parish where the major concern of the parish council at one time seemed to be whether it was appropriate to use parish funds for the rectory secretary to eat a lunch provided by the rectory cook, while she was at work in the rectory. Is this not, the council wondered, an extra payment that is above and beyond the contract negotiated with the secretary?

Both of these stories are examples of democratization and modernization in the use of authority in the Church. One of these approaches works; the other does not. While we cannot disregard the importance of personality here (this bishop would most probably have immediately dismissed anyone who tried to bother him with such trivia about the secretary getting more than her "just wage;" the pastor who let himself get embroiled in the controversy about a secretary's lunch would have a hard time administering a poker club), the issue is more than just the obvious fact that democratic authority requires strong leaders, not weak ones. What was happening in the second story, and is a fundamental misunderstanding among many Catholics today, represents a confusion about what democratic authority is, and, indeed, about what authority is. Unless pastoral leaders, and those who aspire to be pastoral leaders, understand the basis for their power to lead (authority), there is little reason to hope they will be able to administer local churches of the type described in the previous section. Before considering the specifics of pastoral leadership in the parish, we need to consider the issue of authority in the Church.

The idea that authority is the ability to give orders (an idea that is somewhat widespread among certain ecclesiastical leaders, and a portion of clergy and laity in the church today) is theologically, historically and sociologically naive. We will consider a theological basis for religious leadership in a later chapter. Right now we want to examine, from a historical and a sociological perspective, why practically, pragmatically, existentially, and empirically authority has to include the *ability to obtain consent.* The Lord Jesus himself could not get his apostles to do anything on which they had not agreed. Nor can the most oppressive totalitarian regimes govern without some kind of grudging consent. If the governed, if the subjects of authority, if those who must take orders deny the legitimacy of either the orders or the one who gives the orders, then, however theoretically valid and excellent the authority may be, it will practically and empirically have no effect at all.

The order-giving model of authority is still widespread in the church, not because it is soundly based theologically or historically, but rather because it was pragmatically functional for so many years. If a pope or a bishop or a pastor or even a priest gave an order, then it was normally obeyed because there existed a context of acceptance in which people were willing to give their consent to orders passed down by ecclesiastical authority. It is to be doubted that the order was always all that effective, but at least verbal dissent was rarely heard by the ordergivers themselves, however much moaning and groaning there may have been behind their backs. Pierre Teilhard de Chardin went along with the authority that ordered him to silence because he conceded legitimacy to such orders. Hans Kung does not because he does not concede such legitimacy. Athanasius never conceded the legitimacy of the various councils in the Eastern Mediterranean that denounced him, either.

The point of this line of reasoning is that order-giving authority functioned effectively not because of the power of the order giver, or not even necessarily because of the theological or historical grounds for such an approach, but because people were willing to consent to such an exercise of authority, a willingness which has not always existed in the past in the church and which patently does not exist now.

It may be argued that in the order-giving model of the exercise of authority things got done more quickly and effectively than they do now. When the ones in authority, like the bishop in our story, no longer gives orders, things have to be worked out in long tedious discussions in which the appropriate consent is obtained by other means. Still, in a complex world, order-giving only looks efficient. Consider the experience of the Germans in the Second World War and of the United States with the Viet Cong. Pragmatically and practically, the era of instant obedience to orders because the orders were conceded an instant legitimacy is over. If those in positions in authority in the Church wish to lead effectively, they must go back to old, more difficult, and yes, more political tactics to obtain consent. Whether this is a good or a bad thing may be debated; that it is necessary and inevitable, is hardly open to debate. The practical question in the church now is not whether it is necessary to go through a lot of effort, formerly unneeded, to obtain consent, but rather, what kind of effort is appropriate and what matters are legitimate subjects for the quest for consensus.

From a sociological perspective we would say authority is the responsibility to influence human behavior, to motivate humans to behave in certain patterns. Also, it seems that anyone who has authority in the church is commissioned by God, (or by divine delegate) to behave in such a way as to motivate Christians to behave in certain ways and especially to uncover the gospel ways to direct many of these behavior patterns. Indeed, it seems to us that this position is so reasonable as almost to be self-evident. There is, however, a certain kind of cleric (and some non-clerics) who becomes obsessively restless when such a suggestion is made. Those who hold this position are accused of trying to democratize authority or of trying to take away religious authorities' God-given powers.

To this we must say, even the most God-given powers have little impact in the world or on peoples lives unless ways can be found to motivate them to respond to the wishes of those who may have that power. Also, it seems that for over a thousand years church authority was exercised through a deliberate attempt to obtain consent. Even Innocent III, that most imperious and imperial of the medieval popes, did not make decisions without obtaining the consent of the Roman cardinals. Also, for a millenium all major Christian doctrines were issued with something like "with the consent of the whole Christian people." We are not sure how that consent was obtained, but, at least theoretically, it was thought to be there. It seems that the order-giving approach to the theology of religious authority is a shallow theological rationalization for a renaissance model of government, which was a late-comer for the church and which has over-stepped its usefulness, such as it may have been. The order-giving model is ineffective and non-pragmatic. It is also bad theoretically.

Let us consider the approach of the sociologist to the problem of religious authority through an example: you can tell an altar boy to get to church at 6:30 and set up the sanctuary for 7:00 mass. But you can, by no means, guarantee his arrival unless you have motivated him to be there (quite probably you will also have to motivate his mother to get him out of bed so he can be there). A pastor can give orders until he is blue in the face to his associate pastors and other members of the parish staff. They in turn can give orders until they are similarly blue in the face (though to whom they would give these orders these days is open to question) and no one will follow them unless the ones who receive the orders are willing to respond, "All right, I will do it." Virtually the only power left in the hands of the ecclesiastical order givers, having sometime ago lost the secular arm, is the power of the paycheck. Once the clergy become financially independent, there will be no way the ecclesiastical authority can make them do something they have not agreed to do (Hans Kung might not be permitted to teach on the Catholic faculty, but he can still teach; and he is not about to stop calling himself a Catholic just because some people in Rome have decreed that he is no longer a Catholic theologian).

Unfortunately the model of authority as giving orders is firmly built into the structure of the church even though it has lost most of its effectiveness. Even those priests who were trained in the seminary over twenty-five years ago contested the pervasiveness of order-giving and were part of the covert but often highly effective resistence to it. The order-givers were able to maintain external control of human behavior but they were not able to control what people did after they were ordained—as the enormous number of priest resignations shows. Perhaps there is no greater indictment of the failure of order-giving as the model for ecclesiastical behavior than the large number of model seminarians who decamped from the priesthood despite their docility and obedience when they were in the seminary. All that keeps order-giving going successfully now in the church is the checkbook. It may once have been possible to treat the membership, be they priest or laity, as privates in the army. This is no longer possible and administrative disaster is the result of a continuation of such style.

There are at least three reasons why the order-giving model will not work in the church (at the local, diocesan, and world level) today.

1) First of all, this model assumes that the personnel beneath the order-giver are incapable of thinking for themselves. Even worse, it assumes that they are incapable of making a contribution of their own. The one who gives orders thinks he *knows* what must be done. It remains only for the subordinates to carry out those instructions. They have nothing of their own to contribute to the mat-

ter, no insight, no knowledge, no experience, that is of any importance at all. Yet, in fact, the people most familiar with the situation where a decision is to be implemented are those who are actually the closest to the situation. He who governs by giving orders is deprived of the insights, the understanding, the recommendations and the human ingenuities of such people. He is governing, in effect, with one arm tied behind his back.

Father Bill Clark is an avid reader. When he comes across an idea that he thinks would be beneficial for Mary, Seat of Wisdom, he begins trying the idea out on people he encounters at meetings, social gathering, wakes, etc., within the community. Even when he thinks he *knows* that the idea will be beneficial for the parish, if he gets no positive response or even some strong negative response to the idea, he will drop it for awhile and return to it at a later time. He believes that the Holy Spirit has got to help him; if the idea is really worthwhile, in time he will discover people who are willing to respond positively to it. Some of the men in the community remember him mentioning a book he thought they should read and maybe even discuss. Eventually, after he made this suggestion to a sufficient number of men, a few came to one of the associate pastors and asked if they could begin a men's lunch hour discussion group. And, of course, they started by reading the book Bill Clark recommended. Only later did they all begin to realize that the idea of reading the book had been planted in each of their minds by Bill Clark. Other men, who Bill thought would also be interested, were not ready at that time to consider the topic he thought was important. They would not have come to any meeting dealing with the issue, even if Bill Clark had tried to order (something he just never does) them to do so.

2) Next, you can, if you wish, treat a human person like

he is a cog in a machine and if you control him, he will be forced to act like a cog, at least until he can find another source of income. In fact, however, he will resent the treatment you have accorded him and will subvert your instructions whenever he can, not necessarily because he disagrees with your instructions, but because he sullenly resents being treated as though he were a subhuman tool. As we remember when we think of the pre-Vatican II seminary and as we consider authoritarian parishes even today, the one in the position of power may well give the instructions and impose external conformity, but the rank and file have a way of getting even by dragging their feet, by delaying, by putting spokes in the wheel, and by frustrating the authoritarianism of the leader. Remember John Kennedy during the Cuban missile crisis remarking, in astonishment, that he had ordered several months before that intermediate range ballistic missiles be removed from Turkey. "What are they still doing there?" he asked, not understanding the ability of the bureaucratic structure to resist an order of which they do not approve.

In 1980, Cardinal James Knox and the Congregation for the Sacred Liturgy issued a new set of liturgical regulations, most of which reaffirmed existing regulations (which, for the most part, had been ignored by those deeply involved in liturgical "reform"). The regulations dealt with peripheral problems such as communion under both species, communion in the hand, self-communication (a term that one man commented, "sounds like it must be a dirty word") and women servers. The proclamation did not deal with more fundamental questions like the loss of a sense of the transcendent and the bad taste, bad history, bad theology, bad art and music and bad pop liturgical wisdom which had come to be part of the Catholic liturgy.

It simply gave orders. And as such, it was ignored in most places. Parishes where there were women servers continued to use them. The U.S. bishops responded only to complaints they received about liturgical violations realizing, as one bishop commented, "We tell them to stop and they say they will, but they don't." What is a bishop to do? Discontinue all liturgies?

3) Perhaps most important of all, the reasons against order-giving as a model for authority is the fact that, even with the best possible intentions, orders must be passed down through a chain of command and be reinterpreted, retranslated, reexplained, or at least re-transmitted at a number of communication links. A pastor tells an associate pastor something. He in turn tells the school principal, the principal tells the teachers; the teachers tell the kids. In all of these cases there may be sincere good will in transmitting what the pastor has said. But preconsciously, self-consciously, and unconsciously, the instruction is tailored, edited, and reshaped to suit what the transmitter takes to be the situation to which she is transmitting the order. It is a truism of research on hierarchical bureaucracy that orders are frequently, if not always, subverted as they are passed down the chain of command. Not out of malice (necessarily) but rather because with each new transmission there is a different perspective, a different understanding, and a different set of problems.

When one adds to this unconscious or subconscious subversion a deliberate intent to subvert, then the order-giver is in a most awkward situation. Pope Paul VI did issue his encyclical on birth control and right-wing Catholics can probably agree that it was a brilliant exercise of authority. In fact, bishops, confessors, theologians, parish priests, either consciously or unconsciously, but nonetheless very effectively, subverted the teaching of the encyclical. However it may clearly stand on the record as Paul's understanding of Catholic doctrine, it had no effect on human behavior, other than perhaps to turn Catholics against the church's teachings on sexuality. Is such an exercise of authority what is expected of a Christian leader?

Similarly, the Dutch Synod has been loudly cheered as a victory for conservative and law and order forces in the church. But it is reasonably clear that many of the Dutch bishops do not believe in its decisions, that the clergy believe in it even less, and that many of their people reject it completely. The synod then will not, in fact, restore order to the church in Holland, but simply increase the polarization. It will do so in part because there are people in the key links in the communication networks who are bent on destroying the effectiveness of the synod; but also because there are other people who may be less intent on deliberately subverting the synod but whose interpretation of what it means will in fact subvert the intentions of the Pope. An order-giving approach to authority, in other words, which does not engage in the enormously difficult task of winning consent, will not only not work, it is likely to be counterproductive. Perhaps one of the biggest problems faced by Pope John Paul II is that he still appears to believe that ecclesiastical authority enjoys the power it did for a certain time in Catholic history (though not the earliest times nor the longest times)—the ability to give orders without worrying about consent. Whatever the Pope may think, no parish priest or no bishop can afford the luxury of such self-deception.

If one defines authority more broadly (and probably more accurately, historically and theologically, as well as sociologically) as the responsibility to obtain consent, then we may still believe that authority comes from God (as we do), but we also realize that it has to be exercised in very different ways than that with which we became familiar in the church in recent decades and centuries. The person with authority must see himself charged with the responsibility to modify human behavior in the direction of the gospel by providing people with motivation other than the necessarily short run motivations of fear and force.

As we mentioned before, the above definition of authority can scarcely be questioned. If one wishes to have any practical impact, then one must ask oneself what motivations are going to be effective in achieving such an impact. Practically speaking, the only approach that will work is the approach of asking challenging questions and providing a powerful vision of what the goals of the Church and Christian life are. The person who possesses effective authority is not the one who has the ability to give orders, but rather the one who has the ability to ask the most powerful and the most penetrating, most searching, most challenging questions—in part, by the way he behaves himself and in part by the direct and explicit questions he asks and in part by the kind of disconcerting, shattering "stories" he tells. In other words, Jesus' exercise of authority was much more effective because of the stories he told and the deeds he did than by the orders he gave which were, incidentally, few and far between. Washing the feet of the Apostles at the Last Supper was the lesson in the exercise of authority; and many churchmen seemed to have missed it, even though they may now go through the Last Supper rituals themselves at the Holy Thursday liturgy.

One challenges people with questions and provides them with the motivation to modify their behavior in the Christian direction by challenging them more by how one acts oneself than by any instruction one gives. Bill Clark has always believed that a priestly presence in the time of crisis is one of the best ways to assure that those who have severed contact with the Church will be motivated to return. His emphasis on being present at the wake and funerals of all people from the parish in an unquestioning manner (he is known for accepting requests for burial that other pastors might turn down) became contagious. Eventually, all of the parish staff began to see what he meant about the power of grace active in a priest's presence at wakes and funerals. Now the entire staff attends every wake and every funeral. As John Cusick observed, "Imagine what it is like for a family when we all arrive together (as we sometimes do) and conduct a wake service. All the friends and relatives think the family must be quite involved in the Church. And in some instances none of us know anyone in the family."

So it is that the one in authority asks the challenging questions, provides the example, illumines the vision, correlates the Christian message with the world situation and disconcerts those who are afraid of the implications of the correlation. He does not try to force people to do what he wants them to do by threats or fears (Bill Clark never told the others they *had* to be at every wake) or by force or by falling on the sacred authority of his office. He especially does not behave that way now for many reasons, among them the fact that it simply will not work that way anymore (and it really did not work at many times in the past, either).

We need to sharply distinguish between administration, on the one hand, and authority (leadership) on the other. In any properly run organization someone has to be responsible for the bookkeeping and the housekeeping details. Somebody must sign the checks, make sure the insurance is provided and see that the accounting is done.

Someone must buy the stamps, call the boiler repair persons when the machine breaks down on a cold night, see that the snow is shoveled off the sidewalks and the grass is watered in the summertime. None of these things are appropriate matters for lengthy debate or public discussion. It could well be within the pastor's prerogative to say, "I've called so-and-so to bring his plow and shovel the snow off the parking lot." It is not within his prerogative to say that we are going to close the Catholic school. He didn't pay for the school, his children are not going to it, and the fundamental issues involved in religious education are issues about which he ought to ask challenging and visionary questions rather than provide *a priori* and preemptory answers. The middle area between these two is perhaps the most difficult of all. Is it within the pastor's prerogative to say to the associate pastor, "You can't take your vacation during these three weeks because that is when we are having the parish golf tournament." One is dealing here with something more than just bookkeeping and housekeeping, but something considerably less than the ultimate goals of Christianity. Here the example of the bishop, who works out his problems by discussion and consensus and not by trying to impose his own decision, is appropriate.

Note the distinction of three different kinds of decisions referred to above—bookkeeping, housekeeping and administration at one extreme, goals and values at the other, and in between situations and conditions which affect the rights and privileges and obligations of personnel with whom one is working. The administrative trivialities cannot be decided by committee (though they ought not to be decided until after consultation). The goals and the vision—the real authority area of the church—are best exercised the way Jesus exercised them: through challenging vision, disconcerting stories and intense personal examples. The intervening area is the domain of discussion, compromise, consent and broad general agreements that violate no person's rights and with which everyone can live. (Is the associate pastor's presence at the golf tournament necessary because this is one of the only activities for men that this parish has? Has he already had to change plans twice because of the parish mission and confirmation and is this the only other possible time he can find someone to go away with, etc., etc.?) The parishioners who want to argue with the pastor about who shovels the snow should be ignored; the associate pastor who is not giving good homilies should be challenged in a discreet and kindly way by the pastor to improve the quality of his homilies. And the broad questions of how the parish can best use its resources must be dealt with the way Jesus dealt with the broad questions. For example, by stories, by visions, and by challenging, disconcerting and asking questions.

Unfortunately most seminary training in the past (and quite a bit of it in the present) did not prepare people to be talented in any of these skills. Pastors did not learn how to take a firm stand about administrative matters (in which the only final norm is whether the parish stays within its budget and still provides the services most people expect). Nor are pastoral personnel very good at dealing with the complex human issues which surface in matters of performance among professional colleagues.

Nor, finally, were many of them trained to challenge people with questions, stories and examples—the area of religious and ecclesiastical authority par excellence and *stricto sensu*. So it happens that even the young and the liberal pastor tends to fall back on giving orders, laying down the law, and trying to silence the opposition. This simply will not work anymore and fails to accomplish anything.

And here it is that Bill Clark is such a superb example of ecclesiastical authority. He became "Uncle Bill" when his niece, who was then president of the woman's club, introduced him at the first parish function he attended. The name stuck, not because she introduced him in that manner, but because it fits him so well. He is like a caring bachelor uncle, one who is related to and cares for the family, while at the same time he is able to interject an objectivity into his analysis of the relationships in the family. Over time he has come to know most of the people in the parish well enough to know when one or the other is particularly happy or sad. He will stand on the street corner for half an hour "grilling" the eighth grade girls on the latest romances. He will be delighted when a young adult who has moved back to town says, "Uncle Bill, I'd like to go out to lunch with you and tell you about my work." He will drop in for a cup of coffee and only a few months later will the family realize that the seed of the project they are then working on was planted over the cup of coffee. In these conversations he is able to pull back and see problems that are not apparent to the individual families as well as to the "family" of the parish. He seems to love everyone in the parish and in return is loved by them—so when he must challenge, the challenge is given and received in a context of love, not of judgment. And he has a deep, obvious commitment to the Story of God. No one ever doubts the believing basis of all his activities. He has dedicated himself to the parish, because he truly believes that God can be found in the lives of the people and that his role is to facilitate, as much as he can, the discovery of that God.

How is it that a man of his age (he was 70 in January,

1981), educated in a period when priest meant one who could give orders, is able to be the epitome of what we think every pastoral worker should be: a holy person who smiles? The secret to his success, like the success of the bishop in our opening story, is in his respect for people. Unlike the pastor in our second story, Bill Clark is able to love, respect and trust the people he lives with, the people he works with and the people he serves as pastor. Without conscious effort he was able to develop a style of leadership appropriate for this period in Church history (and probably for many other periods too). The skills he has are basic skills that any good leader must have, combined with a love for his religious tradition.

As we consider the principles of good religious leadership from a sociological and theological perspective in the next two chapters, it is important to bear in mind that we think good religious leaders can be developed. Bill Clark might have become one quite unconsciously, but it is possible for young religious leaders to learn from him and to learn the principles of religious leadership his experience calls to mind.

We have a long way to go from the Roman curia laying down orders to pastors asking questions, telling stories and disconcerting by their behavior. Another way of saying the same thing, of course, is that we have come a long way since Jesus of Nazareth, and perhaps only recently have begun to try to walk the path back. Those who decide to walk back on that path will find that the frustration caused when "no one listens to them anymore" is a frustration experienced only by those who still think the way to lead is to give orders.

CHAPTER 7

Sociological Perspectives on Local Religious Leadership

THE type of parish described in the first section of this book, "the parish that works," requires a religious leadership based on pastoral concern rather than on an ability to give orders. As we considered the various kinds of parish leaders we have encountered over our life spans, we concluded that the local community religious leader ought to be a lovable trouble-maker, a neighborhood type with the character to point beyond the neighborhood. He ought to be "a hopeful, holy man who smiles." Precisely because of his smiling holiness, he ought to be able to challenge the people in his community for that commitment beyond the community which hope inevitably demands.

Before addressing the various sociological arguments for this portrait of a local religious community leader, we need to exclude certain issues which tend to confuse many present-day discussions of the social nature of religious leadership. We exclude these issues, at this time, because the purpose of the present study is to uncover guidelines for religious leadership for the here and now—for the 1980's—in Catholic parishes in the United States. For that reason most of our reference will be to the role of priest; not because we do not believe that others in the religious community can and do provide some form of religious leadership, but because for the present time in the Catholic community that it is the role of the priest. If he cannot provide religious leadership then he has no business being a priest. Much of what we say about priestly leadership will also apply to other forms of emerging ministries, but our focus remains on the need to reflect on the actual situation we now face (and are likely to face for the immediate future).

Thus we reject the class conflict approach to local community religious leadership. For at least the last 25 years there has been a recurrent tendency to try to define the role of the ordained minister and the role of other members of the Christian community as in opposition to one another. We know what a layman is by defining what he can do that a priest cannot do and define what a priest is by defining what a layman is not. It is possible to argue that some theological trivia are clarified by this pointless and perennial discussion. But, sociologically, it is irrelevant, historically it is absurd, and in terms of the social policy of the church it is dangerous and destructive. The "divvying up" of work in a parish cannot be answered by *a priori* definition, much less by definitions which seek to limit areas of competence and responsibility as matters of principle rather than as matters of pragmatic practice, a practice that may vary enormously in different times and different places and with different men and women. (A positive description of the interaction of priest and lay person in the socialization process will be found in Chapter 9).

We also exclude the question of the ordination of women, not because we are against ordination of women (we favor it, even more so as we discover evidence of the role a male cleric plays in increasing the marital satisfaction of a man whose wife has been able to confide in a priest; it seems that women priests might perform a similar role). However, we do not anticipate that women will be ordained in the near future. Although we lament this and consider it unjust, we do not think it should keep us from our examination of the social nature of priesthood. When the day comes that women are admitted to the priesthood, we will expect that women who want to be ordained should be "hopeful, holy women who smile." The skills required for successful leadership for a male priest will be just as essential for women in their role in the local church.

Now to the more positive aspect of our presentation: religious leadership (exercised either by the primary leader or by his associates) as an exercise in lovable troublemaking. The kind of leadership described here must be exercised in an effective parish by the pastor, the associate pastors (should the pastor and people be fortunate enough to have such) and by all the professionals who collaborate in the religious leadership for the parish.

We begin with the simple assertion that the people must love their priest. This doesn't mean that they must be happy with him all the time, that they must be pleased with everything he does, or that they must be satisfied with his faults and failings—which, given the nature of the human condition, are likely to be multiple and multitudinous. We simply say that the people must love their priest, if anything else is to matter. He may drive them up the wall on occasion. He may stir up, and probably will inevitably stir up, all kinds of ambivalences. There may very well be people in the parish community who cannot stand him and who would cheerfully provide the nails for his crucifixion. Nonetheless, the people must love him or he is wasting his time.

How does the priest generate love among his people?

The answer is that he generates love the same way any-body generates love—by loving. If a priest truly loves his people, then he will be irresistible; not all the time, and not with everyone, and for some of the people, none of the time. The last thing that some people want is a loving priest. Nonetheless, if the priest really cares for them, his people will not be able to resist him. If, on the other hand, the priest is afraid of his people, or does not like them, or avoids them, or is threatened by them, or cannot stand them, he will not be able to hide this rejection very long, and he will be rejected in return. How many priests (and we include here all parish workers) really love their people? On this we have no data and are not prepared to trust our impressions beyond saying that it seems that many priests are afraid of their people, judge them harshly, want to remold them according to the priest's ideals instead of according to their own needs, and enjoy much more sitting in prophetic judgment on them than actually caring for them, or for that matter, even liking them.

Indeed, many priests might be put off by the seeming exaggerated piety of our assertion that primarily they must love their people. Unfortunately, the pious repetition of this assertion has robbed it, superficially, at any rate, of the power it ought to have. For people are hard to love (even an individual person is often hard to love) and loving the people entrusted to one is an extremely difficult, demanding and sometimes terrifying task. To dismiss the challenge to love their people as trite piety is an all too easy priestly escape from the harsh, compelling, disturbing demands of love which is not a pretty, easy, spontaneous, and pleasant activity.

How does one love? Such a question reminds us of Louis Armstrong's famous comment about rhythm, "If you've got it, you don't need a definition for it, and if you haven't got it, no definition is going to help." The love of a priest for his people is like any love. It must be both comforting and challenging. Husbands and wives comfort and challenge one another in good relationships with the balance between the two appropriate to the circumstances. And so do all other lovers if their love has gone beyond infatuation.

Challenging people is rather easy. Not that all of us do it all that often or all that well. Comforting them is much more difficult because comfort has to be sensitive, respectful, freedom-producing, adult, and self-giving. It does not, by the by, mean slobbering over people. It is especially difficult because if you comfort someone else effectively, you both admit your own vulnerability and indeed become vulnerable yourself. Despite the pseudo-intimacy of gestalt or pseudo-gestalt psychology being vulnerable to other people is a tough, tough business. Yet reassurance is the most important part of any love affair; if one can attribute the word "essential" to any exercise of the ministry, then the comforting role is the most essential thing that a priest does. As Archbishop Bernardin pointed out in a talk he gave to priests in Illinois, we all desperately need encouragement and people especially need it from their priests (and priests from their bishop as well as from their people).

What people want and need is usually much less complex and spectacular than we might imagine. The religious leaders for whom they are really looking are not those who can solve all their problems or answer all their questions. Often they already know the answer; they may even know there is no immediate solution to their problem. More than anything else, they look to those who minister to them for their presence as loving, caring and forgiving people. They want their help in coping with their pain and frustration. They are looking for their understanding; they want a sensitive and consoling response to their hurt feelings; they need the spiritual comfort a priest can bring through his ministry of word and sacrament. They are looking for someone who will pray with them, someone whose presence will remind them that, no matter what their difficulties might be, God really does love them and care for them. They want the assurance that the priest will never abandon them.

Yet, while we well know our own need to be encouraged, many priests seem to be very weak when it comes to encouraging others. There is a lot more to ministry than comforting and reassuring people, but it is not only the best way to begin, it is probably the only way to begin. In the local religious community, the priests (and all who share in the exercise of formal leadership) must first of all primarily and fundamentally be encouragers. Bill Clark's unquestioning response to funeral requests, his presence at hospitals, wakes and funerals, his support for fellow clergy are all the marks of an encourager. If priests do not want to encourage, they ought to find themselves another job.

They also must be challengers. They must be troublemakers because, in addition to strengthening the ties of love and affection within the local community by their encouragement, they must also point to the world beyond the community and indeed to the problems in the community which the members would rather not face. Parishes are parochial by definition. All neighborhoods are parochial, though the parochialism is different. *Ex officio,* the priest is held to call to the attention of his people the opportunities, the challenges, the responsibilities, and the obligations they would rather not see. He must do this discreetly, skillfully, charmingly, and effectively. He is not likely, under normal circumstance, to accomplish it by prophetic denunciation, but he must do it insistently, in season and out.

Father Clark upset many of his parishioners when he allowed the anti-arms demonstrators protesting an "arms fair" at a nearby exhibition hall to use the church for a prayer service, just as he upset some when he allowed supporters of Caeser Chavez to present a plea for support to the parish council. He did not judge or denounce those who opposed him on this, but neither did he back down in the face of threats. So, too, when a family in the parish made it clear that they did not want any black person on the altar for their father's funeral (at that time a black deacon was serving in the parish), the two associate pastors composed a scathing letter to accompany the return of the offering the family had made for the funeral services. When Father Clark returned from his vacation and they presented him with the letter they wanted to send, he offered them an alternative, more low-keyed letter returning the offering, and challenging the family to wonder what was meant by the comment that the priests consider "under the circumstance it would be inappropriate for us to accept this." The people were not being condemned; their action was challenged and the door was left open for them to discuss what had happened with the pastor, which they eventually did. His approach to challenging has always been one of "never attack people; only attack activities that appear off base."

Father Dan Smilanic, an associate at Mary, Seat of Wisdom, has widened the vision of the young people through the trips he has organized for groups of teenagers to Appalachia. In fact, the entire parish community is challenged to attend a situation beyond the boundaries of their everyday experience as various fundraisers are held to pay the expenses of the trip and as pictures and articles appear in the bulletin after the young people return. Mary, Seat of Wisdom could become very insular if the religious leaders were not constantly calling the community's attention to the needs of those beyond the community through the soup line, the parish "twinning" with two inner city parishes, food drives and other activities that focus on needs of its fellow humans that it often ignores.

Parishioners must feel a strong ambivalence about their priest. They must welcome his comfort and reassurance and they must be annoyed, disturbed, upset and disconcerted by his challenge. If all he gives is comfort, he is a Pollyanna. If all he gives is challenge, he will be written off as an insensitive neurotic. He must do both, and indeed do them both in such a subtle way that the people in the parish often find it hard to distinguish whether at any given time he is being lovable or making trouble—partly, one hopes, because he is doing both simultaneously.

Because he simultaneously reassures and disconcerts, the priest is necessarily a character, the kind of person you don't normally run into, somebody you cannot stand and you cannot stand to be without. Come see our parish priest, the kids coming home from college with friends from around the rest of the country say. You should see how cool he is and what a character he is.

How well, in general, are the clergy performing their role as encouraging and challenging leaders? Sad to say, the research data indicates that the clergy are quite underdeveloped in these skills. Only a fifth of the people in the country, only a tenth of those under 30, think they are getting high quality sermons. Only a small minority think priests are sympathetic and understanding—neither very comforting nor very challenging in their daily ministry, if one is to judge by such reaction. What is appalling is not merely the phenomenon of the low grades that the laity gives on performance, but the fact that, despite the virtually universal complaint about sermons in the American Church, no effective organized attempt to respond to this complaint has been developed by the clergy.

A priest might argue that he can comfort and challenge without being a good preacher or a good counselor, thereby ignoring the fact that most of the comforting and challenging he will give out will be in homiletic and counseling situations. There are, as we all know, some priests who become tongue-tied before a congregation but are superb in a one-on-one situation. Generally speaking, however, it is true that the man who has nothing to say on Sunday morning has nothing to say any other time of the week, either.

Some priests are also uncertain about their own leadership role. Is the priest really the religious leader of the community? Now that new ministries are developing, perhaps his role is less than he had imagined it to be when he was educated for his role as leader of the community. To this, sociologically we must respond that we cannot imagine a situation in our society and culture in which the *principal* religious leader of a local community will not be the pastor. This is not merely a function of present canonical regulation, but also of the role expectation of the ordinary members of a local religious community. They simply do not know how to comprehend a situation in which the parish priest is not the religious leader of the community. Nor are they willing to devote much time and energy to finding reasons and explanations for situations in which the pastor does not exercise that primary responsibility (those places that, due to a shortage of priests, are serviced by a religious woman unable to celebrate the Eucharist are seen as exceptions that most people do not want to replicate in their community). It may be possible to educate them into another sort of structure (whether it is desirable or not is another matter). From a sociological perspective we would have to say that such education would involve enormous effort, would require a lot of time, and would probably pre-empt energies, time and resources from all other local religious community behaviors and activities.

Some will say that the only thing the parish priest is really needed for is to say mass and give absolution and perhaps preach the word. He is liturgical leader, indeed, but liturgical leadership does not imply any other kind of social leadership. Though this position has a certain validity as conventional wisdom in pop theology, it does not hold up well under serious theological or practical analysis. If, for example, Edward Schillebeeckx's description of the role of Jesus as the one who presided over the table-talk of the apostolic community is correct, then the contention that liturgical leadership does not imply any other kind of leadership simply will not stand the test of good theology.

Nor does it stand the test of sociological analysis. It is absurd, sociologically speaking, to expect the people in a local community to comprehend that the man who is the liturgical or religious leader of their community has no power beyond saying mass and absolving sins. The laity will not be able to comprehend, nor can they be expected to comprehend, the notion that there are multiple forms of official religious leadership within the structure of their community, and that these various forms are exercised independently of the primary leader of the community. What kind of an organization is that, they will ask and, with every right, be offended and affronted by such chaotic institutional structure.

Practically speaking, those who think the laity easily accept a non-priest in a religious leadership role should talk with the lay people and religious sisters and brothers engaged in ministerial activity or in other church-related work. They recognize that no amount of "expertise" in the area in which they are working substitutes for the "power" (and many times this is in the good sense of the word) the pastor exercises when he offers an opinion on a religious matter (or how often he is expected to offer an opinion, even when he doesn't). At Mary, Seat of Wisdom, where some parishioners feel they should be allowed to help more in certain areas that require "religious expertise," even those parishioners recognize the importance of the leadership of the pastor. They feel that the genius of the parish flows from the leadership style of the pastor. They would like a larger part in sharing of the ministry, but they know very well that their fellow parishioners expect the pastor to be the primary religious leader.

This sociological fact imposes on the primary religious leader of the community enormous difficulties and responsibilities; difficulties and responsibilities that most parish priests are not capable of fulfilling, and hence the tremendous dissatisfactions to parish professional staffs and among the people who are being served by these staffs. The pastor must create a climate and atmosphere in which the professional insight, skills, training, and vision of his collegues will be maximally utilized and developed to their fullest potential. It is an extraordinarily demanding ministry of service. Most priests are not very good at it, were not trained at it, and do not know how to do it. So they choose one of two escape mechanisms. They either become authoritarian and make their own hasty and ill-advised decisions and then impose them unilaterally, or they abdicate all leadership responsibilities entirely and hope that something good will come out of the collective chaos in which their principal contribution is to shrug their shoulders and say, "I don't know, what do you think?" In neither instance is the priest responding to the expectation of the people.

Yet we have argued sociologically that every community needs leadership and that at this particular time in history the laity expect that their primary religious leader will be a priest. Thus it seems mandatory that priests develop the talents needed to be encouragers and challengers.

In conclusion, the "hopeful, holy man who smiles" must be a challenging lover and a loving challenger, and he must be good at what he does. And if a parish priest says, "I am not good at loving, I am not good at challenging, in fact, I am not good at anything," the appropriate response is not to get out, but get better.

Before turning to the specific skills needed for pastoral leadership in the modern local religious community and the educational approach to acquiring these skills, we need to consider the theological character of this religious leadership as well as the relationships between styles of ministry and religious leadership and the process of religious socialization. Questions about these relationships as well as those concerning the role of the priest in the local church and professionalism in the priesthood require the illumination of a religious understanding of the meaning of priesthood.

CHAPTER 8

Theological Reflection on Local Religious Leadership

THERE are, as we noted in the previous chapter, tremendous expectations placed on the religious leader of a parish. These expectations combined with inadequate training have contributed to a situation that can best be described as a crisis in morale for the present religious leadership—i.e. the parish priest. Other factors also helped create this crisis; one which becomes quickly apparent when one converses with those in parish ministry is that there is too little reflection on the character of the kind of *religious* leadership expected of the local priest.

This situation has not been notably helped by theological reflections. There is a widespread sense that the earlier neo-Scholastic and mainly ontological understanding of the role of the role of the priest has now become, however true its ontological conclusions may still be, no longer a functional reality for priests. For an ontology, that distinguishes the "natural" and "supernatural", has ceased to function for many priests as the ethos and world-view it must be in order to empower religious leadership. That scholastic theology-ontology now receives what Newman called a "rational" as distinct from a "real" assent.

The real problem with "rational" assents is that they do not function in any empowering way for a mode of life.

Once (not so long ago, in fact) that ontology did function in an empowering manner. Indeed most of us can recall how well it functioned. We all have those memories (and not simply unhappy ones). We all know that at one time a substantive-ontological understanding of "priest" allied with an understanding of the whole of reality as distinguished into "natural" and "supernatural" orders functioned powerfully and well.

In short, to recall Clifford Geertz's important point on religion: only when the religious person believes that *how* one ought to live *(ethos)* is firmly grounded in the very nature of reality (world-view) does "substantive" religion really function as it should (e.g. "to provide long-lasting moods and motivations with an aura of factuality"). The priest of this earlier model could and did unite a priestly ethos with the natural-supernatural world-view. He could feel, sense, know, through real assent how the *ethos* of his own life and the life of the people was encompassed by an aura of factuality and was grounded in what he firmly believed to be the nature of reality itself. Our memories of the parish priests of our childhood fit this model, with very few exceptions. Their sermons, to be sure, were not memorable (unless one has a taste for mixing the genres of neo-scholastic seminary theology and some "homely" examples). Yet their actions—as believably religious persons and often as *religious leaders*—consoling, comforting, provoking "their" people to the right ethos were memorable and deserve far more honor than the usual "memories" of them allow.

All of this may seem like a rather strange exercise in nostalgia. Yet it is not that, really: we do not mourn, even though we do honor in memory, this "priest of the past" and the natural-supernatural world-view and its attendant ontological-supernatural understanding of priesthood and thereby of religious leadership. Our point is a more general one: viz. that religious leadership can only function as it should—i.e. to empower, evoke, elicit a religious ethos and a religious world-view—when some *substantive* understanding of the religious vision has been internalized with an aura of factuality. The natural-supernatural model of the world (and thereby also of priesthood), despite its grave theological difficulties (on which more below) did function substantively to empower a real form of religious leadership.

Implicit in these comments are several points about our present situation. First, the valuable, necessary, fruitful discussions on the various forms of ministry needed on the local level seem to operate with so heavily a functional notion of ministry that it becomes difficult to see what substantive understanding of religious leadership as religious is operative in that understanding. It is not the earlier natural-supernatural model, but what is it? Perhaps some really religious vision is operative, but little attention seems addressed to that empowering vision. Instead, we focus upon the many new and diverse functions and ministries needed.

In our present, necessarily pluralistic situation, we do not learn to live with, even embrace the real enrichments of what William James named experience itself: "a teeming, buzzing confusion." We do, in short, need more reflections and experiments on ministry and ministries as functional and pluralistic. Yet we also need some more reflection on the religious character of the religious leadership role present in all forms of ministry. This general need becomes intensified, moreover, in terms of the major focus of realistic concern, the parish priest. The major theological need here is the need for a *new* theology of the priesthood where the new formulations of the substantively Catholic religious *ethos* and *world-view* can function again to empower the *religious* leadership role of the priest.

We will not here attempt the full dimensions of this (viz. a substantively new theology of the priesthood). Rather we will concentrate on one aspect of the theological issue, viz. models for *religious* leadership actually operative in the practices and diverse theologies of the priest. We will do so by recalling the classic models of H. Richard Niebuhr on the relationships of "Christ and Culture" in order to suggest the relative adequacy of a model of transformation for religious leadership. The latter model, we will suggest, is both more faithful to the transformative genius of the Catholic religious vision and more adequate as a general model to the many concerns and needs for religious leadership of the priest of the post-Vatican II, American, contemporary complex and pluralistic situation.

Theological Models of Religious Leadership

To recall Niebuhr's models: in determining the relationship between "Christ and Culture" (or between "the source of the Christian fact" and the source of contemporary experience), certain logical possibilities have presented themselves in the history of Christianity. Assuming that the basic *logical* possibilities for the relation of "Christ and Culture" follow the usual logical lines of "all," "some," and "none," one can see how the spectrum emerges. "All" means a model of pure *identity* between Christ and Culture (e.g. Harnack, Ritschl and some of the Catholic modernists). The other end of the spectrum, "none", indicates radical non-identity between Christ and Culture (or between common human experience and Christian experience). It is, therefore, called "Christ against Culture" as its logical opposite, the first model, is called "Christ in Identity with Culture." The classic instance here is Tertullian and his famous adage, "What has Athens to do with Jerusalem?" The "some" possibilities historically encompass three major types: "Christ Above Culture"—the classic Thomist model of the natural-supernatural; "Christ in Dialectical Tension with Culture"—the classic Lutheran model of the "Two Kingdoms"; and "Christ the Transformer of Culture"— for Niebuhr the more relatively adequate model and for us the model that best fits the religious genius of Catholic Christianity and that does seem to fit as a consensus model for a post-Vatican II substantive religious and theological vision.

It may seem somewhat peculiar to appeal to H. Richard Niebuhr's models for the relationships of Christ and Culture throughout the entire history of Christianity (Catholic, Protestant, and Orthodox) in order to try to illuminate the question of religious leadership in one Church-tradition, our present Catholic one. Yet our strategy—and risk—is perhaps worth noting explicitly; first, if we focus on the religious-theological side of the "religious leadership" question, then precisely some general models for the substantive religious vision (ethos and world-view as they relate to contemporary experience) are needed to inform the wider discussion. Second, our belief is that contemporary post-Vatican II Catholic Christianity shows the presence of all five models in different concepts and practices of religious leadership operative in the church. If the latter belief is true, then one aspect of the "religious leadership" question is to focus on whether there is a relatively adequate general substantive model to inform the discussion. Such at least is our present strategy and risk.

First, please recall the comments from the beginning of this chapter. The earlier model of the "natural and supernatural" orders informing earlier religious and theological ontological understandings of priesthood is based on the scholastic model of "Christ Above Culture." It is, in fact, this model which has collapsed on us. Even Thomas Aquinas (Niebuhr's example) did not necessarily hold it— at least not if Karl Rahner's reformulation of the nature-grace distinction in Thomas is correct. Recall, that for Rahner, and most contemporary Catholic theologians, *grace* is *the* concrete ("all is grace") and nature is a "remainder concept"—i.e. an abstraction from the concrete to allow one to understand a possibility, not an actuality. Yet whatever the truth of the interpretation of Thomas himself, the early, pre-DeLubac, pre-Rahner Thomists did hold to a "Christ Above Culture" model. That model formulated crucial distinctions between two *concrete* realms (one "natural" and one added to the natural as "supernatural") as its operative theological vision and informed the operative ethos of Catholicism (e.g. supernatural as distinct from "merely" natural virtues).

The functional temptations of this inadequate substantive theological model seem clear enough: first, the "natural" is at once downplayed as "merely natural" and overextended from an abstract possibility to the "concrete" realm. Second, the powerful post-Vatican II vision that "all is grace" and our concrete experience is always graced is rendered inoperative by the belief that grace is a reality *added to* the really concrete, nature. Third, the "Christ Above Culture" model informing a notion of priesthood can too easily slip into that great vice of our tradition—a clericalism which finds itself religiously and theologically reinforced by a "Christ Above Culture" model and becomes "The Priest Above the People" model of clerical lore. These three temptations of the classical scholastic model remain only that—temptations, not necessities—as our earlier comments on the fuller complexity of its often humane, priestly, non-clerical functioning among the "priest of yesterday" may suggest.

And yet these temptations are rooted in the fundamental theological inadequacy of the model itself. For Catholic Christianity, as Rahner and most contemporary Catholic theologians hold, is, on present terms, a model of "Christ transforming Culture" not "Christ Above Culture." That transformation model is the religious and theological vision most needing incorporation and internalization into contemporary models of religious leadership. But before speaking explicitly of that, let us turn to some brief comments on how the other three models (Christ in Identity with Culture; Christ Against Culture; and Christ in Dialectical Relationship with Culture) seem operative in some models of post-Vatican II religious leadership.

1) *"Christ in Identity With Culture"*: This model seems operative in any form of religious leadership where the Christian gospel no longer bears any prophetic power but simply reenforces some dominant secular world-view. The pure "psychologizing" of the gospel into purely private, self-fulfillment trips of a narcissistic sort are the most obvious example of this. The rate at which sermons can become, not application of the liberating, provocative, judging and healing message of the gospel to our contemporary personal, social, and cultural experience, but

merely a kind of popular psychology decked out with a few New Testament proof-texts is another illustration of the theme. The strength of this model is its legitimate and necessary desire to apply Christianity to contemporary experience by means of the insights of psychology, etc. Its weakness—a fatal one—is that, rather than studying possible identities, continuities, and non-identities on a case by case basis, one assumes an identity and moves on.

2) *"Christ Against Culture"*: This model of religious leadership seems to assume that a truly prophetic or even apocalyptic stance demands that the real religious leader *confront* the people continuously with their "sins" or their society's and culture's "sins." As with the first model, this assumption proves so general that a case by case analysis does not actually function. The strength of this model is its insistence that a prophetic, confrontational, exposing moment is central to the Christian gospel and that the concern for social justice is not an avocation but a central calling to every Christian religious leader. Insofar as this model operates well as a central reality in every religious leader it sensitizes the whole community to the confrontational, prophetic core of the Christian gospel. When it operates alone as the sole vision of what religious leadership means the same model can harden into a self-righteousness beyond the horizon of even an earlier clerical culture and approaches the model of the religious leader as ayatollah.

3) *"Christ In Dialectical Tension With Culture"*: This model, although less frequent among Catholic priests than the other four, does occasionally surface. In its Catholic form, it can surface as a kind of separation (including, of course, some unresolved dialectical tensions) between one's calling as a priest and one's calling as a modern pro-

fessional. One lives, in a sense, in "two kingdoms"— priest and professional (of whatever sort). One also lives with the constant danger of sentimentalizing the first (the priest as "nice guy") and separating that priestly role from one's second, professional one (the competent, "hard-nosed" administrator, teacher, professor, etc.). The strength of the position is that the tension is recognized and, if intensified and reflected upon theologically, can lead to real efforts to relate those two "callings" in a complex world—priest and professional. However, when that reflection begins in earnest for a Catholic religious leader who takes the Catholic tradition seriously, a move will be made to a transformation model. We realize that a Lutheran minister in fidelity to her/his heritage may work this model out on its own terms more fully. But we suggest that a Catholic religious leader who has experienced the collapse of the earlier "Christ Above Culture" model and the distinct but real strengths and weaknesses of the "Christ in Identity With Culture" and "Christ Against Culture" models may well experience the dialectical tension of this fourth model but will want some more intrinsic relationships between these two roles (priest and professional). Thus will one move forward to reflecting upon the model of "Christ Transformer of Culture."

4) *"Christ Transformer of Culture":* A model of transformation suggests that the fundamental relationship between "Christ" and "culture" (or our Christian experience and our common human experience) is one in which Christianity transforms an already basically trustworthy human experience in the light of the Christian symbols. Sometimes, in fact, the transformation works the other way—as in the use of the natural sciences, the social sciences and history to transform the interpretation of a

traditional Christian symbol (e.g. creation) in the light of contemporary knowledge (e.g. evolutionary theory). The logical model for a theology of transformation is one where individual theologians and religious leaders establish mutually critical correlations between the meaning and truth of the symbol of faith and the meanings and truths of our contemporary experience.

That general model, therefore, is a general model that informs but does not determine particular cases. Each case needs the discernment and further reflection of the religious leader to see how the transformation works in this particular case or how the correlation is to occur in this case. In short, in principle, sometimes an identity between Christian and contemporary experience may be present. At other times a confrontation (especially of a prophetic sort) is needed. At still other times, continuities, similarities, likenesses, analogies and differences are present to aid the transformation of our experience (e.g. of the stages of life) by the Christian symbols (e.g. the sacraments).

We have shifted Niebuhr's own mode of transformation to our own model of correlations between the Christian symbols and experience. In this model in the Catholic mode, analogies are usually anticipated although both identities and radical non-identities (prophetic confrontation) are sometimes needed. In general, the Catholic religious and theological vision is a transformative one whereby Christian experience (e.g. of love as gift from God—agape) tranforms and sublates but does not negate our ordinary experiences of love as striving, desire, *eros*.

Let us restate the beliefs expressed earlier in this chapter in this new "transformation-model" context. First, the mainline Catholic tradition, despite the neo-Scholastic "Christ Above Culture" model of the late nineteenth and early twentieth centuries is a "Christ the Transformer of Culture" model. Thereby does the tradition encourage the religious discernment and theological articulation of critical correlations of our ordinary experience and our religious experience. Ordinarily, this religious vision anticipates that the symbols will experientially transform but not negate our ordinary experience. The Catholic religious leader who ignores this empowering Catholic religious transformative vision is likely to ignore such positive realities as an already existing community, an already existing goodness, decency and love, a real sense of justice that needs encouragement and occasional confrontation but not self-righteousness.

To confront while comforting, to console while allowing the wider vision to transform, to heal while prophetically confronting, to search for the analogies in our common and trustworthy experience to which the symbols do speak—all these concrete realities are evoked, elicited, empowered by the *ethos* and *world-view* of the Catholic transformative religious vision of reality. The contemporary religious leader should know this as naturally as the priest of yesterday knew in his bones the "Christ Above Culture," natural-supernatural, model. The contemporary Catholic religious leader, thus understood, will know instinctively that continual self-transcendence, transformation, is what individuals and communities need as a model to live by—not the easier and less complex models of popular psychological self-fulfillment (Christ in Identity With Culture) or the clerical instant-answer-man (Christ Above Culture—the priest above "his" people or the constant confrontation of every self via authentic prophetic righteousness and anger become clerical self-righteousness against the people.

By all means, the Catholic religious leader, the priest, needs to bring the prophetic witness to bear upon himself and the parish by recalling the gospel call to social justice. By all means, the Catholic religious leader needs to turn to psychology and every other helpful discipline to aid him in helping the symbols of faith really disclose their experiential power to our ordinary lives. Yet these two crucial tasks are best done in fidelity to the transformative religious vision of Catholic Christianity and in harmony with the "correlation" model of contemporary theology only when the full range and power of the "Christ the Transformer of Culture" model is internalized by contemporary priests as well as the "Christ Above Culture" model was internalized by the priests of yesterday. For that new substantive religious and theological model, that *ethos* and that worldview, will free the religious leader to discern religiously and reflect theologically upon the real complexities and greater possibilities of this latter day given to us as gift and command.

CHAPTER 9

Local Religious Leadership and Religious Socialization

AT this point in our examination of leadership in the local religious community we need to move from a sociological and theological analysis of the role of the priest as religious leader to a consideration of how the pastor and his associates are in fact (even though not always consciously) performing a particular leadership role. The pastor and his associates are expected to perform a certain role. The process by which the people in a community reach a point of expecting this from their pastor is closely connected with the process of socialization we noted in our previous discussion of the importance of local community. At various points in the socialization process the people in a religious community look for leadership and expect that their priest will be the one to give it (although they might not always be aware of why it is that they look to the priest for this leadership, they still do).

As we analyze the process of religious socialization we discover a relationship between it and styles of religious leadership and ministry. We now need to consider the role of religious leadership in the socialization process from early childhood through the early years of marriage. This examination is largely speculative since there is little data from which to proceed, but it intends to point a way that priest-leaders might begin to examine how they actually do function in their religious communities. We will also discuss some models of ministerial style each of which has its own set of properties and potential impact on the socialization process (most of these models are being practiced presently, though the ministers might not be aware of it). We will conclude with an examination of natural ministerial activities which leads us to speculation about the two-way flow of the socialization process.

Childhood Through Early Years of Marriage

Much has been said about socialization in childhood and the various kinds of effects which adult behaviors have on children. This is a time during which children internalize values and come to see them as their own. In our society this period runs from infancy through adolescence and the internalization varies accordingly. Infants tend to internalize images and sensations and as they begin to grow they begin to put together a value system from all the pieces they have been absorbing. This latter part of the process continues at a decreasing rate for much of adult life.

Previous research has shown that father's religious behavior and mother's religious joyfulness have strong effects on the religious behavior and imagery of their children. People whose father was devout tend to be more devout themselves, and people whose mother approached religion with a spirit of joy tend to have warmer images, especially about Mary, than those whose mothers were not joyous. These socialization effects also have their impact on religiosity in later life as the child grows older. However, there is no information about the role of the religious leader in this process, so at this point we will be engaging in speculation about what that role might be and what its effects might be.

Part of the ambiguity in this exercise is asserting just who the local religious leader is. In some ways we would like to think of the pastor or perhaps on occasion the associates. However, for the purposes of discussing socialization a little clarification is in order. Children operate with sets of symbols for religion. They know little of theological issues and they know even less about internal Church politics or even parish politics. They internalize stories and try to make the real world around them fit the information contained in the story. At least for most children, the parish church and the pastor represent the symbol of religion in their lives. The school is important and the principal of the school, if she is a nun, might have a heavy dose of religious symbolism about her, but she does not have a church and people don't seem to be relating to her on Sunday. That is why the pastor and his building are important, because they have no real competition in the eyes of the children.

For many children the buildings of a parish are actually their first religious socializers. Some pre-schools take children on a tour of the church as part of their introduction into the mystery. One teacher claims they are more impressed by that than by anything that is said during the year. (The most revered object was, by the way, the red fire extinguisher enclosed in its recessed glass case; this always fascinated them.) They seemed to understand that this is a special place where important things happened. The priests, especially the pastor, are special because no one stopped them from going anywhere they want to in this special place. (Of course later on the problem becomes one of convincing people that the priests do not own the place; but then that is a problem with some priests as well.)

Children internalize religious symbols from their earliest years and the importance of these first contacts should not be ignored. They know that the Church is important enough to have its own big building. They know that people seem to behave better around there and that it is usually neat and clean. (Neat and clean means a lot to children who seldom are.) They also know that this all has something to do with God and his relationship with us.

The real problem facing religious leadership is what do they do with this initial symbolic internalization. Priests, especially pastors, are almost as important to children as buildings; they start off with a positive reaction from children simply because they are attached to the mystery of the church. What do they do after that?

At this point we come across the first problem that most priests have with regard to their role as religious leaders and socializers—they do not understand that they are mysterious symbols to children. They do not take full advantage of the fact that children react positively to them as religious symbols. Instead they fail to really think about children much at all, preferring to work with the adults in the community as counselors and managers, and sometimes as prophetic challengers.

Children tend, all things considered, to like priests. They like to have them come into their classroom because it means school, which is boring, stops for a while. They like to have them come into their homes because they will have something special for dinner and mom and dad will not pay much attention to what they are doing afterward since they will be in talking with Father. (Of such opportunities much can be made!) Children may not like priests for all the "right" reasons, but why look a gift horse in the mouth?

Unfortunately too many priests fail to recognize the power in this initial "liking" of the child. They dismiss them as just the kids, instead of thinking how they might be able to use these positive reactions to build on. At the outset, priests might be thought of as "sort of like God" by many younger children. This tends to make priests uncomfortable as if the children really would continue to believe it. Instead, it should be seen as the beginnings of a symbol system which would become enormously complex, but which would incorporate the image of the religious leader in a role of central importance.

The power of the priest to motivate religious symbolism can be very great, but only if the priests themselves are aware of it. The priest who fails to realize that he is a part of the child's symbol system, misses the first crucial step in being an effective part of the religious socialization of that person. Empathy, likeability, challenge and "the storyteller" are all qualities or roles which are part of religious leadership in the local community and they begin in childhood perceptions. Leaders who do not sense that never get beyond the authority and managerial portions of their jobs, portions which are really quite unimportant to average persons and their religious needs.

It is difficult to go jumping about the life-cycle as if there were clear, distinct areas with neat gateways and boundaries. The movement from childhood to adolescence and young adulthood can be very subtle and the religious issues which accompany that motion are not less so. However, the early years of marriage do bring a new awareness and perception of the change in life-cycle periods, and people do sense that they are no longer the ones who are cared for but that they must now do the caring. The same issues which apply in childhood tend to apply in the same way during adolescence. Religious leaders who perceive that they are liked and that they are part of the mysterious story do well with teenagers; those who want to deal only with adults do less well.

However, once people have been married for a few years and begin to realize that they are in a trough of sorts, they need to be able to get in touch with their symbols of hope and transcendence and they once again turn to religious leaders for some idea as to how to do that.

We know that people tend to have declining rates of marriage satisfaction for the first five to eight years after the wedding. We also know that for many there is an up-turning in these rates beginning about the eighth or ninth years. Young married people need to find out about this and there are several reasons why. They begin to think that the dreams of their youth cannot come true and that they will never be as happy as they once thought. They have begun to take each other for granted and the needs of job and family have intruded on much of their available time. The days go by and then the months and years as well, and they wonder why it all seems to pass so quickly. Religion, which may have been appealing in their younger days, now seems filled with rules and meetings and endless committees where responsibility is to be shared but nothing very satisfying ever gets done. At some point in this litany of woe they begin to think about the symbols of hope and caring love which they associated with the church as children.

Unfortunately, the symbols do not mesh anymore and the impression is left that religion, too, has become stale and has lost its ability to renovate. Many priests come across as questioning more than the laity do. It is not that people want specific answers, they simply want to rehabilitate the feelings and convictions that within their religious symbols an answer lies somewhere in the future. The dormant symbol system does have images of caring and warmth and loving hope which can be called on in times of doubt and fatigue, but there is no one to help the process along when the leader is in the midst of his own crisis or, worse yet, simply too busy with meetings and managing the parish to be attentive to these needs emanating from the experiences of his people.

And so it continues throughout the life cycle: people encounter moments when they have a need for the message of God's gracious love to transform their situation. The priest who has developed a style of ministry that allows him to be an agent of that transformation process, both by his comforting and his challenging, will find that he is in accord with the ethos of Christ as Transformer. He will be very much in keeping with the classical tradition of Catholicism, even though he is acting in a ministerial style quite different than that of the previous generation of parish priests. At the present time there are a variety of ministerial styles being practiced by persons serving in some type of pastoral leadership role.

Models of Ministry: from the Traditional to the Uncharted

The six models of ministerial activity presented here are intended to be descriptive of the ministering which is currently being done and are meant to be neither exhaustive nor mutually exclusive. Some individuals will perform several of these functions while there may be others who are considered as ministers who perform none of them.

The purpose of the models is to organize our reflection on what we are now doing and the needs which are being fulfilled.

First are the *Keepers of the Institution.* These people may be ordained or non-ordained and they administer, direct and consult with the various bureaucratic church offices at the local and the national level. Their function is primarily the maintenance of the institution and their greatest needs are informational. They must develop positions on many topics and they represent the institution in the larger socio-political arena. Currently there are not very good mechanisms for getting these people the information they require and, as a result, they tend to become insular and preoccupied with institutional concerns, rather than with issues to which the institution ought to respond. Their theoretical operating base is more bureaucratic than theological and the danger in their ministerial lives is failing to see the forest because they are worried about the declining number of trees.

Next are the *Evangelical Recruiters.* Evangelization has come to be defined in a variety of ways from proselytizing the "unchurched" to bearing witness within the family and the parish. The recruiters' primary need is an audience to listen to the evangelization process. Many of them are quite undaunted by the evidence which suggests that, for Catholics at least, no such audience readily exists, and that the traditional forms of evangelization are really quite foreign to most who would enter the Catholic church. This model of ministry is marked by enthusiasm and eagerness, both of which are positive and necessary characteristics today, but it is also marked by a reluctance to listen to the people one is preaching to, a liability to which we will return to in the next section.

Two kinds of "helpers" comprise the next two models of ministering and the first of these is the *Secular Helper.* (Secular in this context refers to the nature of the "helping," not the status of the helper.) This type of ministry is increasingly common in the parish, on the campus and in various diocesan social service settings and it focuses on the communication and therapeutic skills which are commonly used to help people in dealing with psychological and emotional problems. A variation of this kind of ministry can be found in those who, through the application of organizational skills, help communities and parishes state their goals and articulate their visions. While there is no doubt that these have been useful skills to acquire, they also contain within themselves a subtle seduction of self-perception. The practitioners of these trades can fall prey to defining themselves only in the context of immediate problem-solving, ignoring the theoretical underpinnings of their work and the ultimate purposes to which the immediate solution applies. For example, we teach people to communicate with each other with skill and we help them organize their parish meetings so they operate efficiently, but frequently the system breaks down as people begin to ask "why" they are doing these things. The question of purpose cannot be answered without reference to an underlying theory.

The second kind of helper, the *Pastoral Helper,* attempts to respond to this need for theoretical support, usually through the application of theological insight and reflection. The usual method of the *Pastoral Helper* consists of working from the important experiences of people through the application of the Christian tradition to the experience and arriving at a plan of action derived from the self-understanding which is promoted in the lives of the people being helped. From a sociological point of view the important property in this style of ministry is the opportunity to listen to the lives and experiences of people, and to interject into those phenomena the insights of the religious tradition. The great need within this model is the theological expertise and the skill at interjecting it in a profitable manner. Given the harsh blows dealt theology by the "relevant revolution" of the past decade or so, such skills are currently difficult to come by.

A fifth ministerial model is that of the *Liturgical Celebrant,* and this comprises the celebration of the Eucharist and the leadership of the liturgical community. Most often this role is reserved for the ordained priest, but non-ordained persons are finding themselves more and more involved in both the celebration and leadership functions within parishes and other forms of religious communities, and many priests seem to find this model either too narrow to exclusively occupy their time, or too unchallenging to fully occupy their energies. This is the most traditional model of ministry and it is also the one about which we are currently most uneasy; we really do not quite know what to do with the powers hidden within the celebration or with the potential for leadership which resides in the person who leads the liturgical community. Sociologically these are very strong symbols, but we do not have an equally strong theory which guides our use and development of these same symbols. We knew what the role of the celebrant and leader was in the immigrant model of Catholicism, but we are unsure of it in the post-immigrant era.

The final model of ministry, the *Ministry of the Laity* (as opposed to lay ministers), is the most elusive of the models because it is moving into uncharted territory. We have had lay ministers for many years in one form or another, but there has not been an attractive, well-articulated theory or description for the ministry of the laity that was specific to the lay life and not derived from principles established for clerics and religious. There is virtually no theology for the lay vocation and the various offerings on the "priesthood of the laity" have been ignored or uncomprehended by the vast majority of lay Catholics. Rather than trying to place an existing model of ministry on top of the laity we might better assume that lay Catholics are acting out a ministry experientially and our task is to discover the key elements in those experiences and help people to articulate them within a framework consonant with the Christian tradition. The result might be a flourishing of a variety of ministries of the laity, many of which people did not even think to call ministry. The realization that they had been acting as ministers might also compound their self-identity as witnesses, Christians, and people whose lives are turned toward God.

However, in order to discover the ministerial experiences in the lives of the laity, we need to listen to them in a systematic way and to have respect for what we hear. In the following section we will discuss a few examples of the contexts in which ministerial activities emerge—if we are willing to look and listen for them.

Natural Ministeries: A Context for Listening

The initial stance of the belonging minister is listening. The pastoral minister must listen not only to what is said but to what, even though it is unsaid, is felt. Listening, in the sense of entering into and understanding, is not an innate disposition in humans. It is a discipline that must be developed against the constant preoccupation with the self and its thoughts. One of the hazards of ministry is that the

169

minister reads too quickly the needs of the people. He does not listen, he guesses and his guesses often reflect more of himself than actual community needs. He begins to build programs and services around these guesses and is painfully surprised by the fact that very few seem interested. (See: John Shea, *An Approach to Pastoral Theology* for more on this.) Not only are personal and community needs reflected in the process of sympathetic listening, but the ongoing ways in which people minister to each other naturally are also revealed. These natural ministries provide an opportunity for the Church to enter and illuminate the lives of people and to help them foster their own sense of efficacy as ministers and develop skills which build upon the natural base.

There are many contexts in which natural ministering occurs, but four of the most general are the family, work, community and Church. There are ministerial activities which occur in each of these settings but, more important, there are, inbedded in these experiences, opportunities for the emergence of ministries which are truly appropriate for the laity which only need listening and reflection to be revealed.

Opportunities within the family are related to the ambiguity of intimacy and the dynamic of parents and children moving through the life-cycle. Husbands and wives minister to each other when they help one another to grow within the paradigm of sexual intimacy, although few understand that this is a ministry because seldom has it been explained to them as such. Children and parents minister to each other as they mutually socialize each other into specific value systems, but they have seldom heard the term "ministry" used with regard to themselves. The extent to which people in religiously mixed marriages take advantage of their opportunities for ecumenical ministry is unknown because the Church has never made a study of the subject, but it is likely that a portion of that population has had experiences which are very instructive in this regard.

The ministerial nature of "grass roots" activity in the context of people's work is even less developed than that in the family. The opportunities are there in such issues as the establishment of priorities, the use of time, satisfactions and accomplishments and failures all of which provide natural settings in which people can minister to each other in helping and/or reflective ways. However, unless there is developed a theory and a theology of work which incorporates the experiences of the people, the opportunities for ministry will be wasted. People need to be able to place their helping and reflective behavior in a religious context and give it meaning beyond the immanent if they are to begin to build a self-definition as minister which is genuinely "lay" in nature. Work has been dignified by our social theology, but it has yet to be examined as a paradigmatic experience which can be the source of theological reflection and religious development.

Another locus for the development of a genuine ministry of the laity and the skills of religious reflection is the local community or neighborhood. When we consider the neighborhood aspects of local religious community we open whole vistas of ministerial opportunities for lay people. If the local church encapsulates the whole mystery of the experiences of people at that level, this ought to provide rich materials for the expansion of the concept of ministry. Neighboring, socializing, helping, coffee-klatches, political activity all become infused with a ministerial character and therefore become elevated in the religious self-consciousness of the community and the individuals.

A final context for natural ministry can be found within the institutional church itself and that it is in probing and recognizing events and moments of intense religious insight which happen rather frequently in the lives of ordinary people. One conclusion of the recent research into the prevalence of mystical and ecstatic experiences done at the National Opinion Research Center is that they are much more common than many people thought and that they occur in the lives of ordinary, non-clerical or religious people, people with no advanced religious training. An exploration of these experiences may prove enlightening to those interested in the relationship between faith and everyday living. The opportunities for ministry range from assisting people to understand the nature of such experiences so they are not frightened by them, to the articulation and nurturance of such experiences so that they may contribute to the ongoing process which is the unfolding of the religious heritage at any one point in time. If those who are fortunate enough to have these experiences feel that their stories will not be respected, they will be lost to the community. If, on the other hand, the language of mysticism becomes available to a wider audience, more and more people will benefit from such insights and the context for natural ministry will be expanded.

Socialization in the local religious community can occur at many different times and places. The interaction between leaders and people within different styles of leadership is a reciprocal process. Leaders are only effective when they become adept at listening; and the people are only able to expand their own religious lives when they become adept at providing some leadership. The socialization process, which begins as a one-way flow in childhood, quickly becomes two-way as the internalized symbols and values of the leaders and their people interact on the local scene. The local religious leader must learn both to recognize his character as a recipient of the positive, hopeful symbols which have been internalized since youth, and to listen for the ways in which adults try to renovate their symbols when they need them. He is involved in both kinds of socialization and is also socialized himself by such experiences. In this analogy, religious leadership is learning to walk both sides of the street without getting totally lost in the neighborhood.

As the priest walks both sides of the street he discovers that giving orders is not the way to lead people who are looking for the transformative power of a religious message. He also quickly learns that part of his leadership role is to encourage natural ministries as they surface within the community. The move from a world-view of Christ Above Culture to one of Christ As Transformer of Culture leads the priest from a role of Priest Above People to one of Priest as Encourager and Challenger of People. As encourager and challenger the priest also discovers he must be willing to share a good deal of the ministering function of the religious community with other professional ministers as well as with the natural ministers of daily life. Many priests find this need to share ministries causes confusion about their own role. We now turn to an examination of how the priest functions as religious leader in the local church where new ministries are evolving.

CHAPTER 10

The Role of the Priest in the Local Church

THE confusion of most priests today is captured in this story: In 1970, at a workshop on the role of the priest in the local Church, one priest scrawled a question mark on his name tag. When asked who he was, he shot back, "How the hell should I know." Now as we enter the 1980's that priest is probably still out there. He lives in a rectory and works hard at what he does. He has had a relatively good and constantly busy ten years; but he has never taken that question marked name tag off his black suit. His real name is legion.

There is a definite, and at times screaming, need for theological and operational clarity with regard to the role of the priest in the local Church. But whatever theological vision of priesthood is articulated, it must fight mightily against rhetorical flourish. Language about priesthood tends to fly high, escaping the world of doorbells, phones and angry people for a more rarified spiritual atmosphere. Lamenais' type cant about a "heart of flesh for charity and a heart of iron for chasity" quickly insinuates itself into conversations and drags priesthood into sentimental piety. At the present moment priestly bombast, no matter how inspirational, only deepens the malaise. And whatever operational definitions of priesthood may prevail, they must be sufficiently concrete to enable priests to try them. General statements about priesthood may be helpful as guiding convictional and value remarks, but they must be supplemented by concrete renditions of what a priest does and how he does it. In other words, both theological and practical understandings of priesthood must be grounded in the actual conflicts and possibilities of a priest's life as it is lived day in and day out, in the environment of the local Church.

Any understanding of the role of the priest must be articulated in direct dialogue with two current "state of affairs" in the local Church. The first is the emergence of new ministries. The second is the "devalued feeling" about priestly ministry, particularly priestly ministry at the grass roots level.

Ministry is an exceedingly difficult word to pin down. At one time it suffered from underuse, referring almost exclusively to the work of priests. Today, the problem seems to be overuse, referring to anything anybody does. Brian Joyce speculates: "Ministry can easily become the most hackneyed term of our decade, and it can be used in such a general sense that it applies to everything everyone does and, in the long run, to nothing of significance" ("Ministers and Ministries: Sharing An Understanding," in *Parish Ministry,* Vol. 1, No. 3). James Coriden has a similar worry: "Ministry . . . is somewhat of an endangered species—it's liable to be used so generically and so vaguely as to lack all meaning, to lose all distinction" ("The Permanent Diaconate: Meaning of Ministry." by Rev. James Coriden in *Origens,* Vol. 7). The emergence of new ministries may unintentionally submerge the term.

One set of distinctions which seems to bring order into the formlessness of ministry has been suggested by the

Asian Colloquium on Ministries (*Origens,* Vol. 8: No. 9). First, they distinguish between services and ministries. Services are "those ways of sharing the church's ministeriality which are undertaken spontaneously and on occasions." Ministries apply to what "church members undertake with a certain stability and exercise on a sufficiently broad basis, thus sharing formally in the Church's responsibility to signify the presence to men of Christ's saving action." Secondly, ministries are divided into those conferred by ordination and those conferred by installation. Ordained ministries are the espiscopacy, priesthood, and diaconate. Installed ministries will depend on the needs of each particular community and the number and type will differ from place to place. The Asian Colloquium elaborates thirteen. A few of them are: evangelist, ministry of family apostolate, ministry for youth, ministry of social concern, ministry for education. These particular installed ministries would resonate with the emerging ministries of the Church in the United States.

Accompanying this expansion of ministries is a popular understanding of Church which legitimates it. The Church, especially the local Church, is viewed as one charismatic whole. By virtue of baptism each person possesses gifts for the building up of the whole. Although not all of these gifts will develop into definite ministries, the recognition of the "total giftedness" of the community situates all ministries in the broadest base possible. There is no preeminent ministry, whether it be bishop or priest, which the other ministries merely share in. Each ministry ultimately grows out of baptismal inauguration and has its own integrity and life source in the needs of the community. In other words, to place the discussion in the context of the immediate past, the multiplicity of ministries is not "helping Father out" but ministries in their own right.

It is within this milieu, and out of this ecclesiology, that the role of the priest must be specified. The immediate suggestion is that ordained ministry is for the purposes of pastoral leadership. Bishops and priests exercise pastoral leadership; deacons exercise pastoral assistantship (Cf. Richard McBrien, "Service + Mission = Ministry," *Today's Parish,* October, 1979). On the parish level, the priest is either a pastor, associate pastor, co-pastor, or in some teams where the term pastoral is applied to the entire staff, the priest is designated by the specific tasks he performs, e.g., financial liasion, religious education liasion, etc. Each of these terms connotes different sets of relationships and different responsibilities. At the present moment, the theory and practice of these diverse possibilities for priestly ministry has not been thoroughly sketched out. Yet, it seems that Nathan Mitchell's general focus would apply to the ministerial role of the priest no matter how it is nuanced: "To oversee and coordinate the ministerial gifts of the baptized and to preside at those public moments when such gifts and services are corporately expressed through ritual" ("Ministry Today: Problems and Prospect," *Worship:* Vol. 48, No. 6).

These twin roles seem a step in the right direction. Priesthood and liturgy are historically and logically linked. On the parish level, to be a priest is to be at the center of the liturgical expression of the community's faith. Also a parish of many ministries will mean someone will have to act as a unifying and coordinating force. The priest meets with the various ministers and resources and coordinates their efforts. In the language of systems design, the priest acts as a consultant to a group of mediators who will deliver services to a target group. The priest (consultant) meets with the ministers of care (mediators) to talk about how to visit people in the hospital (target group). The priest (consultant) meets with five couples (mediators) to plan a marriage preparation program for engaged couples (target group). This does not eliminate one-to-one ministry on the part of the priest. But it does indicate a greater amount of time and energy will be spent in empowering the ministry of others.

This initial chiseling out of the role of the priest is not sufficient. It is often too quickly and inaccurately translated into the tasks of administration and liturgy. The priest deals with the logistics and bottom line problems of the other ministries. He is brought into the conversation with "Father, do you think we can get the money for that?" or "Will the parish council go along?" or "Why does the choir always get the hall on Saturday? Can they move to Thursday?" The overseeing and coordinating function collapses into strictly managerial shuffling. Also, for the priest, liturgy (outside daily and Sunday eucharist) can become a "hireling" task. When various groups within the parish—CCD classes, discussion groups, teen retreat days—want a mass, the priest is contacted. The liturgy is geared around a small group (but the celebrant has not been a part or only sporadically a part of that group) with common experiences (only the celebrant has not shared those experiences) in an informal setting (only the celebrant does not know the names of half the people). This not infrequent situation is particularly ironic. The war cry of the late sixties and early seventies was that the priest is not a Mass machine. But with the proliferation of ministries and the consequent rise of small groups combined with the dwindling number of available priests, the priest often has the feeling of being a liturgical night rider. When priestly ministry moves between the poles of administration and liturgy, it becomes a disjointed surface, and increasingly frustrating experience.

The second factor in the atmosphere of the local Church is a "devalued feeling" about priesthood. Whereas the emergence of new ministries can be verified by statistics, this "devalued feeling" is more difficult to delineate. It is a mood, an underlying attitude, which at times is explicitly dealt with; but which, for the most part, remains beneath the surface while business as usual goes on. It is shared by both priests and non-priests.

On the non-priest side, a distinctive shift in perception has taken place. At the beginning of the "changes in the Church" era, the non-priest world of the local community saw the priests as the instigators of the changes. They questioned, "What does all this mean?" and "Why are you doing this?" The answer ranged from rambling explanations to dumbfounded silence. It only gradually dawned on the local congregation that nobody held the reins, least of all the parish priest. Today the parish priest is often seen not as the initiator of change but its victim. In many cases the laity and the new ministries have adapted more quickly than the local priestly leadership. The ironic result is that groups within the local Church talk of "bringing the priest along" and "he's getting better" and "we have been trying to educate him liturgically." No matter how priestly leadership is defined, it must be a vanguard rather than a rearguard position.

Among priests themselves the "devalued feeling" has many causes. The ones most frequently mentioned are: lack of support systems among priests; living day in and day out in conflict situations within the rectory, with the people and with higher Church authorities; the tension that exists between what the role demands and what the person believes; the resignation of fellow priests; the decreased number of seminarians; the lack of collegiality in decision making; celibacy becoming a countersign, not of commitment but of loneliness and frustration. Underlying these immediate influences is a theological shift that is often not focused on. The close and almost exclusive bond between priesthood and salvation has been broken.

The rectory conversation runs:

1st Priest: "How come so few confessions? Are people sinning anymore?"

2nd Priest: "I think they think they can get forgiveness straight from God."

1st Priest: "Yeah, but only with a perfect act of contrition."

2nd Priest: "That's easier these days."

1st Priest: "Where does that leave us?"

No matter how you would want to question the assumptions or change the direction of that conversation, one perspective would remain. Both technical theology and popular cultural mood maintain that God is present in the ordinary events of human living. While the sacraments may be "guaranteed encounters" or "full and explicit" encounters with God, they are not the exclusive locales of divine activity. In theological jargon the incarnation and the sacramental continuation of that event is placed within the universal presence of God to his creation. Grace is coextensive with creation and so God and his forgiveness are available in the most unsuspected places.

"Where does that leave us?" is the cleanest expression of the priestly problem. Every priest over 35 once wrote that he sought ordination to save his own soul and the souls of others. The way he saved the souls of others was through the administration of the sacraments. The holy oils were in the glove compartment of every car and no accident was ever passed by. A sacrament could mean the difference between eternal damnation and salvation. Naturally, the man who brought the sacrament was extremely important.

At first glance a widened understanding of God's salvific activity seems to diminish priesthood. With the sacred permeating the context of the secular and the secular the sacrament of the sacred, divine activity can be readily contacted independent of the seven sacramental channels. Ordained priesthood appears to lose its power and purpose. In this theological framework the sense of being at the center where all things hang in the balance disappears from priestly lore. The extravagant claims of bringing God to people yield to the more modest proposal of uncovering the God who is already there. The sacraments and the priest who brings them do not insert God into the situation but reflect the God already active in the situation. This shift may seem slight, but its initial impact is large. Salvation and priesthood are not exclusively bonded. The result is that the role of the priest appears diminished.

It is within this atmosphere of multiple ministries and devalued priesthood that the role of the priest must be theologically and operationally delineated. The way of "overseeing and coordinating" must be spelled out so that (1) it creatively interacts with the other ministries and (2) it is integrated into the traditional concern of the priest with the salvific movement of God. Liturgical celebration must grow out of the total priestly task and not appear as an isolated island of mystery in an ocean of middle management concerns. Although the focus of these reflections is priestly ministry, it must be remembered that clarity for any one ministry means clarity for all.

Faith Reflection in the Local Church

There is Reason, asserting itself as above the world, and there is Reason as one of the many factors within the world. The Greeks have bequested to us two figures, whose real or mystical lives conform to these two notions—Plato and Ulysses. The one shares Reason with the Gods, the other shares it with the foxes.

Alfred North Whitehead

By etymological definition and historical precedence, the priest minister deals with the mediation of the sacred. The locale of his ministry is the movement of God in people and the movement of people in God. If this movement is wider than sacraments, then so is the priestly task. The emphasis on the universal presence of God does not lessen priesthood but refocuses it, freeing it from a narrow liturgical-sacramental definition. But unless the priest can name and celebrate the non-liturgical activity of God with the same precision he can name and celebrate the liturgical activity, this new focus and the possibilities it brings will be lost. The most immediate task of priesthood is to develop ways of attending the ubiquitous presence of God.

A most functional approach to this understanding of priesthood is to say this priestly ministry insures that the fundamental convictions and values of the Christian faith are related to the ongoing concerns of the community's life. The convictions and values of Christian faith are truthful embodiments of the God-humankind relationship. If we view life through these lenses, we will be attending to the divine lure present in the situation. Therefore, the priestly ministry encourages the correlation between faith and life. The priest is a resource to groups and individuals so that the behavior they are engaged in has a faith motivation and the area of life they are dealing with is appropriated from a faith perspective. The priest is explicitly concerned with the faith identity of the local Church.

Whenever the other ministers hear a role definition of the priest minister they have sharp ears for one thing. Is he on my turf? An initial response to that question is to return to the ecclesiology of gifts in a very fundamental way. All ministries are outer oriented. They are meant to insure that the community engage in certain activities. They are not the personal possessions of individuals but services to the larger community to facilitate and be a resource to its life. Certainly a dimension of all ministries (youth, liturgy, social action, religious education, etc.) is the relating of faith convictions to the task at hand. All ministers will be engaged in that reflection as part of their work. It is not necessary that this be done *by* the priest (this is seldom advisable) or *with* the priest. It is what the Christian people do as they go through life. However, the theory is that the priest, because of training and experience, will greatly enrich the process and bring theological depth and traditional backing. His presence to the other ministries and to any group or individual means that the faith convictions and values are going to explicitly enter the discussion. This is the specific way he "oversees and coordinates" the ministerial gifts of the community.

This is a fine distinction but an important one. The priest is not the exclusive "faith reflector" but his specific ministry is to insure that faith perspectives are neither ignored nor contradicted. In other words, priestly ministry encourages the priestly task of the people. In fact, the purpose of every ministry is to elicit the specific character of that ministry in the community. At this point in the history of parish staff development, the scriptural text that hangs in the meeting room should be Luke 9, 49–50:

> It was John who said, "Master, we saw a man using your name to expell demons, and we tried to stop him because he is not of our company." Jesus told him in reply, "Do not stop him, for any person who is not against you is on your side."

All ministries live in the tension between usurping the task and seeing it is done.

The task of faith reflection, which the priest facilitates and funds with resources is a combination of reason above the world and reason within it. As the Whitehead quote suggests, it is the mission of the god and the fox in each person and in the entire community. The god in us constructs the fundamental meanings which act as the permeating context of all thought and activity. It considers the question of how our ultimate beliefs influence our proximate worlds. What does the compact phrase, "God is love" look like unfolded, in this home, in that neighborhood, in your work? The fox in us carries the agenda of this faith into action. It is our shrewdness and ingenuity to create structures, programs and systems which make convictions concrete and values effective. Faith reflection is a wholistic enterprise, engaging mind, heart, and action. It is a never-ending dialogue between the god and the fox.

The priest facilitates and is resource to the task of faith reflection in various environments. In pastoral ministry, environment is the key factor that determines style and method. In general, four environments can be distinguished. Liturgical environments, in particular eucharistic celebrations and within that the homilectic reflection, is one locale—and many think the most important—where the priest relates faith and life. A second environment is the one-to-one setting. This would include counseling, spiritual direction, and in some cases individual convert instructions. A third environment is reflection groups without a communal task. Examples of these would be scripture study groups, prayer groups, CFM, pre-Cana, Marriage Encounter Weekends, etc. The individuals within these groups may leave the group with personal tasks to be accomplished but the group as a whole does not act together. The fourth environment is task-oriented groups, e.g., ministers of care, parish council, liturgy teams, planning groups of any sort. These people are participating in a ministerial task and must work together to accomplish it.

The way in which faith reflection goes on in each environment is different, and not to be sensitive to this diversity is to be ineffective. In a homily the priest by himself (except when there is a group effort) engages in the faith reflection for the community. While this is appropriate in a liturgical setting, it would be disastrous in a reflection group. A priest who monopolizes the faith reflection produces dependency in some people and anger in others. In a one-on-one setting where the faith reflection is often very personal, the priest might share at some depth his own struggles of faith. While this might be a creative response in a conversational setting, the same self-disclosure might be out of place in a liturgy. Furthermore, a short homily given to a task-oriented group usually both impedes the task and obstructs any real consideration of how faith convictions might influence what must be done. One of the more pervasive, but unsung, problems of priestly ministry is a monolithic method and style which is appropriate in one environment but which, when transplanted, works against genuine faith reflection. What must be developed are diverse methods and styles which respond creatively to the diverse environments of priestly ministry.

Summarizing our reflections on the priest-leader up to this point, we find that the role of the priest in the local church is one of leader of the religious community, encourager and challenger of all he encounters, proclaimer of Christ the Transformer of our human experiences and faith reflector for the particular community he serves. Our priest with the question mark might be experiencing confusions because this vision of priesthood demands knowledges and skills that were not part of his priestly preparation. Quite simply, seminaries have not prepared priests for the type of ministerial leadership needed in a religious community at the present time, with the result that there is little appreciation of the professional competencies needed to perform the priestly task in a manner that is satisfying for both the priest and the community he serves. Priests will begin to discover who they are when they begin to appreciate the various dimensions of the priestly task and acquire the diverse styles and methods which respond to the various environments they encounter.

CHAPTER 11

Local Religious Leadership and Social Justice

CHRISTIANITY, as a religion, includes two major expressions: proclamation and manifestation. Our earlier analysis emphasized the model of "manifestation" for understanding the religious import of sacrament, liturgy, the ordinary-as-extraordinary and the local church. This emphasis on manifestation (or sacrament) has been the genius of Catholic Christianity as a religion, just as an emphasis on the power of the proclaimed word has been the genius of Protestant Christianity.

If Catholic Christianity is to remain faithful to its rich heritage of various expressions of religious manifestation (everyday experience, local community, tradition, liturgy and sacrament), we need, as we have insisted throughout this book, to develop further creative expressions of manifestation on every level of parish life. Since the Second Vatican Council, however, the reality of proclamation has also played a greater and much needed role in the theology and the actual practice of Catholic Christianity. The need for better proclamation—as a crucial example, for better sermons on the parish level—is merely the clearest expression of this reality and this continuing need.

However, yet another biblically grounded religious reality, the reality of the prophetic word and spirit, has also increased its force and power among Catholic Christians. Sometimes this power (as at Vatican II and since) has been directed principally at internal church reform. As our earlier discussions (especially on authority and leadership) make clear, the authors of this study strongly endorse all movements of responsible internal self-reform of the church in every sphere of the church's life.

Yet a religious-theological commitment to greater concentration on the preached word and an increased emphasis on an internal church reform forces the greater realization that the Christian prophetic spirit demands as well constant attention to social justice. For social justice, as the Synod of Bishops declared for all Catholics, is a constitutive dimension of the reality of all Christian life. We cannot only be "seers" of the ever emerging manifestation of God in our life as Catholics nor merely "hearers" of the proclaimed word, we must also become "doers" of the word through concrete actions for social justice at the parish level and beyond. Even when we cannot agree with some of the concrete proposals of the present "liberation" and "political" theologians, we must all join them in their correct theological insistence upon the demands of the prophetic word upon our actions and thoughts for all the oppressed and alienated. For all oppressed persons and groups remain "privileged" to the Christian prophetic conscience just as those "unprivileged," forgotten ones remained the ones most "privileged" to the great prophets of the Old Testament and to Jesus himself. Christianity is not a religion which is concerned only with "private" matters between the individual and God. Christianity must be a public reality, for Christianity attempts to aid all authentic causes for justice in both the church and the wider society.

Parish Leadership and Social Justice

Since the local parish is almost inevitably the arena in which motivation for social concern and social action are learned, the local religious leader is almost inevitably the principal agent in presenting the Church's social commitment and motivating lay people to honor that commitment. Such statements are certainly indisputable psychologically and sociologically, and also theologically sound. On some occasions one has the impression that certain of those committed to social action would oppose the local religious community to the broader concerns of the Church and write off the parish as "parochial." We think that this opposition is unsound, if not dangerous. The local community is a necessary base for social action. The two fields of religious endeavor compliment each other instead of being opposed to one another.

There are, of course, some Christians who sustained a profound and authentic social commitment which was neither learned in a local context, nor is supported presently by a local community. It is no criticism of such individuals to say that most people will learn that the Church has a social perspective only in the context of the local community and will not become socially committed and involved unless and until they receive powerful support from that community.

Psychologically, we believe that such an assertion is beyond question. The dangers of fadism or adolescent romanticism or superficiality for the "lone wolf" activist are so well known that they need not be detailed here. Sociologically, as we have pointed out repeatedly in this book, religion for most people is a matter of home, family and local neighborhood. If they do not hear about social justice and are not motivated to pursue the quest for social justice in their religious community, they will obtain knowledge and motivation nowhere else. Theologically, it would seem that social involvement will be the result of hearing the word preached and participating in the Eucharist celebration, both of which, in the normal course of human activities, occur in the local religious community.

The leader of such a community, then, is the absolutely essential and indispensible "gatekeeper" through whom the social vision of the larger Church obtains access to the Church's ordinary members. If he doesn't preach it, and if he doesn't practice it, the social gospel of the Church is not going to be heard.

He must, however, be very good at preaching it and very faithful about practicing it. Through the years the laity has acquired a profound skepticism of clerical claims to expertise in the world beyond the boundary of the Church. The research evidence available to us demonstrates that the laity are as skeptical about the clergy's right and capacity to preach on social questions as they are about the clergy's right and ability to preach on sexuality. All too often it seems to many of the laity that the clergyman simply does not know what he is talking about when he preaches on race or economic or international justice or the third world or the rights of women or multinational corporations or consumerism or any of the other evils on which the clergy, hierarchy, and occasionally even pontiffs, pontificate so easily. If priests tell the laity, for example, that the poor nations are poor *because* the United States is rich, or that it is unjust that America should use half of the world's natural resources (without mentioning that America also feeds half of the world and that the exchange of natural resources for manufactured goods is simply foreign trade), the laity will not believe them. The clergyman with simple analyses, easy answers and moralistic self-righteous solutions to complex human social and economic problems rapidly loses all of his credibility. He is asking for a new form of clerical distance. He demands that he be dispensed from professional competency because he is a clergyman. He is arguing, at least implicitly, that his Roman collar, his clerical credentials and his *ex officio* position as a minister of the word give him the right to propound solutions to such problems without having to study them and understand them, and without any need to acknowledge the complexity of such problems. The local religious leader, in other words, can make no claims which will be honored as a social analyst or a social critic simply because he happens to be a clergyman. Unless he knows what he is talking about and can demonstrate the validity, complexity and sophistication of his knowledge, then he will do more harm than good, for he will demean the Church's social message, caricaturize it, and discredit it. If he cannot demonstrate to his congregation an ability to be nuanced, sensitive, moderate and sophisticated in discussing matters of economic and social justice, it would be much better if he said nothing at all.

Unfortunately, there is not now available for religious leaders the resource data which would enable them to be well informed on the complexities of social problems or, indeed, to understand how one might respond to such problems out of the perspective of a Catholic/Christian social ethic. There are no longer "authorities" who play the intervening role between theory and practice that were once played by men like John A. Ryan or George Higgins. A major gap in the training and resource supply of local religious leaders is the absence of program and publication on Catholic social theory and practice. A quarter of a century ago such facilitating resources existed. They no longer do. It is beyond our capacity in the present volume to outline a new program that would enable local religious leaders to exercise a ministry of raising social awareness and increasing social commitment in their congregations. We must be content with pointing out the need for such resources and warning that uninformed and unnuanced cliches about social problems in the Sunday homilies are dangerously counterproductive.

However, the local religious leader should be aware that there is no such thing as *the* Catholic answer or *the* Catholic solution or *the* Catholic program of social action. There are, rather, Catholic answers, Catholic solutions and Catholic programs about which men and women of good faith, good will, integrity and intelligence can legitimately disagree. One may, for example, cheerfully denounce the multinational corporation. Yet it could easily be argued by those whose social commitment is no less authentic than the critics of the multinationals that if all such corporations were destroyed today, others would have to be invented tomorrow because they play an essential function in the international economy. Or, one could insist vigorously on the need for a new international economic order, but scarcely be able to refute the contention of most experts in international economics that such an order ought not even be attempted unless the southern hemisphere nations are willing to commit themselves to a program of internal redistribution of wealth, without which any transfer of funds from north to south will be counterproductive for the ordinary people of the southern hemisphere countries. One merely has to mention such complexities to indicate how totally unqualified the typical local religious leader is to speak with the voice of a prophet on such matters. The prudent Sunday homily will refrain from offering cheap and easy solutions and concentrate on trying to persuade the congregation of the complexity of the problem and the need for Christian concern and Christian expertise in seeking solutions. Encouraging young people to prepare themselves academically to meet these problems would be most helpful.

Three Principles of Social Justice

The priest would also be wise if he was aware that there is a Catholic social ethic. There are three fundamental principles in this social ethic which are as anathema to liberal capitalism as they are to Marxist socialism (which in these respects, at any rate, is nothing more than a deviant or heretical version of liberal capitalism):

1. *Personalism.* The principle of personalism contends that the dignity and the freedom of the individual human person is the only justifying goal of the social order. Society exists despite what the Marxists and the capitalists might say to promote the welfare, the wellbeing and the growth and development of the individual human person, and that person may not be sacrificed for any social good no matter how great.

2. *Pluralism.* Against those who wish to bring all institutions of the society under the control of the state, or make all institutions subservient to large corporations, or who see in their social theory no intervening group between the individual and the state, Catholic social theory argues that

in healthy societies there proliferate—often a messy, disorderly proliferation—intervening groups which have an independence and right of their own and which exist neither for the good of the corporation nor the good of the state. Thus, wise social leadership seeks to promote and develop such organizations as family, neighborhood, local community, work group, trade unions, religious groups, fraternal organizations, ethnic collectivity, all of which in the free and independent exercise of their rights facilitate the growth of the individual and welfare of society.

3. *Subsidiarity.* The third principle of the Catholic social ethic which summarizes and applies the first two principles and which contains the genius of Catholic social thinking is the so-called principle of subsidiarity, articulated definitively in the encyclical letter of Pius XI, *Quadragesimo Anno,* in 1931: nothing should be done by a larger and higher organization that can be done as well by a smaller and lower organization. It is the principal call for localism and decentralization and articulates the conviction that small is beautiful and that no organization should be any larger than is absolutely necessary to do the job involved. The locus of control in any human structure should be placed as close to the individual member as possible: nothing done by the international community that can be done as well by the independent nation; nothing done by the nation that can be done by the state; nothing done by the state that can be done well by the municipality; nothing done by the city that can be done as well by the neighborhood; and nothing done by the neighborhood that can be done by the family.

In a church that is changing as rapidly as the Catholic Church is, the local parish provides a point of stability and a point of contact with the past that enables change to occur with less disruption, fear, and alienation. Many commentators within the church see parochial life as being a narrow, particularistic and confining force within the church. They maintain that people cannot be concerned about the global problems of the church, nor can they be concerned about the less fortunate in other lands, nor can they be concerned about the struggles for liberation from oppression in other lands if they are so closely focused upon their own narrow community interests. This point of view reveals a romantic and unrealistic definition of human nature. Humans are social animals; as a result, they tend to live in closely bonded groups when they can. This gives them the strength to go beyond their own survival concerns and begin to think about larger questions, without the close personal bonds forged in social communities, human beings tend to become atomistic and, as a sociologist would term them, anomic. They lose the sense of belonging that their social nature requires.

In human community, particularism and universalism are clearly joined. It is only when we are comfortable and secure in our particularistic communities, such as urban parishes, that we can look with objectivity and compassion upon the situations of other people. An excellent example of this on the current scene is the conflict over the parochial school system.

The parochial school system is perhaps the greatest achievement of the American Catholic Church. The immigrants built the schools to preserve their culture and the faith. Parochial schools provided an alternative to the discrimination the immigrants felt in the public school systems. Gradually, the clientele of the parochial schools changed, so that today it is no longer the immigrants who populate them but the children of immigrants or the children of the children of immigrants. The goals of the schools have changed, too. No longer is it the narrow focus of preserving the immigrants' faith but rather a true concern for developing Christian perspectives in the modern world.

However, the enemies of particularism see the Catholic schools as evil. We are accused of providing schools for white parents to use to avoid sending their children to school with blacks. This stereotype exists even though the data show the contrary. Most Catholics live in areas that are at least partially integrated. Most Catholics send their children to schools that have at least some black children in them. Catholic schools are probably less lily-white than most other private schools in the country.

The distinguishing characteristic of Catholic schools is that they are responsive to local control. There is no large Catholic school board in the Archdiocese of Chicago that makes policy for all the neighborhood schools and that insists that all the schools abide by the same set of rules. Rather, policy is set down by local boards of education residing in each parish. This method has the advantage of utilizing local talent and local resources rather than alienating them. And all this goes against the conventional wisdom that bigger is better. Bigger may be better in terms of lowering the cost of producing automobiles or lowering the cost of delivering food to people, but it is not necessarily better in all things. The parish school functions out of a vision of the Catholic social ethic.

Every pastoral leader should, therefore, encourage the discussion of these Catholic principles of social justice which are functioning in one area of Church life and of the reality of prophetic discernment by the community of

the calls to justice within the parish itself. Equally important, every pastoral leader should attempt to discern how
the prophetic call to social justice can best be met by communal actions for causes, groups, and persons not within
the parish boundaries. The struggles, for example, of
black Americans, the struggles of women worldwide, the
concrete struggle for justice in Nicaragua, Poland, Chile,
the Philippines or Northern Ireland (to recall some obvious situations where the Catholic justice tradition is
fighting often for its very life in concrete and concretely
different circumstances) demand the attention of all Catholic parishes. The attempt—the communal parish
attempt—to find concrete ways to aid the cause for justice
in the parish, American society, and world needs the aid
of both serious and tough-minded reflection and prophetic
discernment.

As in all other matters, we must find on the parish level
better ways to aid one another in this process of real conversation, reflection, discernment. The complexity of the
issues cannot become an excuse to ignore them or to ignore our responsibility, as committed Christians, to aid in
any way we can as individuals, or better yet, as a community. We can be aided in this process of communal reflection by the principles of the Catholic social justice tradition and by encouraging a heightened consciousness
among us all of our responsibilities to the forgotten unprivileged ones—the ones privileged to the prophets and to
Jesus.

The present book is not the appropriate place to lay out
a detailed hermaneutic on the principles of a Catholic
social ethic, much less to articulate an elaborate defense of
or detailed social program based on them (for an exercise
of this sort, see Andrew M. Greeley, *No Bigger Than*

Necessary). Indeed, it is a sign of the times that we deem it necessary to include these three principles in the present work, since a quarter of a century ago one would have taken it for granted that those concerned about local religious leadership would already know them. It suffices to say that in the present context the three principles, especially the last, are a profoundly radical dissent from the conventional wisdom of both socialism and capitalism, and represent an original and authentically Catholic (not uniquely Catholic) approach to social order. The Catholic social theory has a special contribution to a comprehensive social dialogue. If it is not understood and preached by the local religious leader, the Catholic contribution is not likely to be made.

The local religious community must be a sacrament of social justice, not merely in that the social contributions of the word of God are preached in the parish, but also, and perhaps more importantly, in that the principles of justice and the Catholic social ethic must be manifested in parish life. If the abuses of multinational corporations are attacked, but parish employees are not paid a decent wage, the local community is a poor sacrament of social justice. If human dignity and freedom are strongly endorsed, but parishioners and parish staff are manipulated and used, then the cause of social justice is not well served. If the rights of women are stoutly defended, yet the women in the parish, whether on the staff or among the parishioners, are treated like second class citizens, then the principles of feminism will not be heard by the members of the Sunday congregation no matter how strongly they are intoned from the pulpit on Sunday morning. The Gospel of Liberation will be attended by ordinary parishioners only when they perceive that their religious leaders have been liberated from the hang-up of authoritarianism which often plagues those who are most liberal in theory.

Liberation occurs first of all in the imagination, in the preconscious, in the stories men and women tell about the meaning of their lives. Resistance to oppression as a Christian obligation and privilege is perceived first of all on the level of the story, the image, the picture. The story that a parish tells about social justice in its daily life and in the ordinary dealings of the leadership with the people of the parish is a far more powerful feature of social justice than the propositions concerning social justice that the parishioners hear from the mouths of their parish priests. It is much to be feared that the greatest temptation to violate social justice that the parish clergy must resist is not the temptation to obscure the Church's social ethic lest the parishioners be offended by its demands, but the temptation to violate that social ethnic in the style in which the parish is led; for the authoritarian leadership style is deeply ingrained in clerical culture and has historical roots which reach far back into the past. It is almost the "normal" style of parish leadership, the pattern into which priests fit without having to think about it. Even if their ideology is liberal, they are still severely tempted to force their parishioners to respond to or to parrot that liberal ideology—for their own good, of course.

As a good rule of thumb for the leader of the local religious community, he is proving a poor sacrament of the Church's social ethic whenever explicitly or implicitly he tries to force virtuous behavior, social or personal, on his parishioners, either explicitly or implicitly on the grounds that he is forcing this behavior for their own good. In the pre-Vatican II Church, the paradigmatic oppression was forcing children to go to confession on Thursday before

First Friday in order that they might develop virtuous habits. That particular form of oppression may no longer be widespread, but more subtle variants of the same paradigm continue to exist and are especially pernicious when the behavior demanded, perhaps subtly, is behavior that objectively conforms to the liberal agenda.

While we present a separate chapter on the social justice dimension of parish life because we believe that no discussion of the training and function of the local religious leader can afford to omit this critical dimension of a church's mission, we, nevertheless, insist that the social commitment of Catholic Christianity is not a separate aspect of parish life, but a dimension of the parish's transparochial obligation and commitment which ought to mark every aspect of parish life. It ought to permeate into parish community both in its internal functioning and its external vision the same way that incense used to permeate the sanctuary during Benediction of the Blessed Sacrament.

CHAPTER 12

Professionalism and Local Religious Leadership

DURING the period when the world-view of "Christ Above Culture" resulted in an understanding of priesthood as "Priest Above People," there was little emphasis given to a need for professionalism among priests.[1] A priest was talented because he was a priest. After surviving the rigors of seminary life and an education with a heavy diet of a philosophy and a theology that made little attempt to be open to the experiences of the people of the day, the priest was considered to be fully prepared for the task ahead of him. The fact that we have good memories about many of the men we encountered in parish experiences in the past is a testimony to their ability to be men for their times without (and often even in spite of) a preparation in their seminary life. And continuing education for the priest working in a parish was not given much attention. What did the priest have to learn? He had completed his seminary training and that was all that was necessary.

This attitude toward the priesthood as a vocation that did not require any professional standards and for which a priest was completely competent at the time of ordination has continued to plague the present-day priest. Calls for professionalism in the priesthood are more often than not viewed as somehow contrary to the notion of priesthood as a "religious" vocation. Yet it is this very lack of skill and art that contributes to the sense of confusion represented by the priest with the question mark. If there are no theories of priesthood against which standards for priestly behavior can be set and preparation and continuing education programs can be designed, then there is also no need for the priest to be concerned about accountability. Yet where else do we find young people entering a career at age 25, and never again being subjected to any meaningful critique about their progress? In such an environment it is little wonder that so many priests are unsure of who they are and what they should be doing.

At the risk of being called heretical for considering that something more than the grace of the sacrament is needed to assure good priestly leaders, we would like to examine the present state of the priesthood as a profession, compare some of the problems encountered in the priesthood with similar problems in other professions and then turn to a consideration of how the ministerial leader functions with the other members of the ministerial team. Much of what we are saying in our analysis of the present state of the disciplined skill and art of the priesthood is negative because, unfortunately, as the identity crisis of many priests indicates, there was little in their seminary training that would allow them to grow and develop the disciplined skill and art needed as they moved through the various stages of their work. Until there is a widespread recognition of the need for skill and art in the priesthood, many priests will continue to fail to re-tool as they encounter the need to acquire new skills. They will, in short, continue to be unprofessional and continue to wonder who they are.

First, some reflections on the skill and art of the priesthood (in the narrow sense of the ordained clergy).

1) The disciplined skills and art of the clergy are sadly underdeveloped. As mentioned earlier, the laity give priests today low ratings on the quality of their sermons and on their behavior as sympathetic and understanding individuals (two areas that would seem to be part of the priesthood no matter what our world-view would be). And there has been no effective organized response to the continuing complaining of lay people regarding the poor quality of both sermons and behavior. Protestant ministers, who come from a tradition that emphasizes proclamation more than manifestation and analogy, consider the Sunday sermon an indication of how well they are performing their ministerial role. Many are responsive to criticism by the congregation, and give a considerable portion of their working time to preparation of a good sermon. The poor quality of many homilies in Catholic parishes emphasizes the need for increased attention to the importance of proclamation. The lack of individual and group response to improve this situation indicates a problem within the profession.

2) Unfortunately, it is not an exaggeration to say that many priests do not read much and that some priests do not read at all. The anti-intellectualism and the lack of education among the clergy might have been tolerable three decades ago when our population had less education than it does now, but it is certainly not tolerable now. If so many sermons sound like the priest has nothing to say, the reason is that he does indeed have nothing to say and he has nothing to say because he hasn't thought seriously about anything for a long time, and is still leaning back on his seminary notes for his religious ideas.

And little is done to mitigate the problem of undereducated clergy in all too many seminaries today where most emphasis is on pop psychology and ministerial skills (often unrelated to any theory of ministry) and very little emphasis is placed on thinking, writing or speaking.

In what other profession can the phrase, "I don't know much about—scripture, theology, sociology of religion etc., etc."—be considered not only an excuse but a positive endorsement of what one is going to say? Somehow it would seem that for many of the clergy being undereducated is, far from being a vice, reckoned positive virtue.

3) We do not know of any other professional group in the country where envy is used so effectively or so systematically to punish excellence and reinforce mediocrity. Any priest who does anything even moderately unusual or gets any kind of even modest acclaim for something he has done is almost certain to have the powerful sanction of clerical envy imposed upon him, and not subtly or discreetly as happens in all other professions, but openly, obviously and explicitly.

We are not suggesting that all priests, or necessarily even a majority of them are unskilled, undereducated and envious. What we are saying is that the culture and structure of the clergy as an occupational group is permeated with an indifference to skill, a contempt for education, and a positive hostility to excellence or acclaim.

Those negative professional behaviors are often a defense against the feelings of helplessness priests experience as they encounter some of the inevitable obstacles of their limited attempts to practice leadership in today's parish. So many people are into being ministers these days that they often feel obsolete. Why should they bother trying to be professional? They are not even sure what they should be professional about.

It sometimes helps if we can place ourselves in a larger context so that we see that the problems or obstacles or challenges which we face are not ours alone but ours shared by a number of different occupations or classes of people. With regard to the new self-awareness in ministry, there are parallels in other organizations, particularly business organizations, which are instructive. Many businessmen today complain constantly about the number of meetings that they have to attend and the general low productivity of those meetings. Seminars in communication skills and interpersonal skills are an attractive market for business organizations. Executive seminars are the order of the day in many of the Fortune 500 companies because they have found that their managers do not know how to communicate ideas and organize activities productively. Many of these same business organizations are also facing greater specialization and compartmentalization which makes the need for communication even greater.

Another obstacle which many in the ministerial life find challenging is the tendency to become cynical in the face of unsuccessful programs and efforts. This, too, has its parallel in many other kinds of voluntary programs such as the Peace Corps and ACTION programs or radical change groups. People in these kinds of groups have for many years expected great changes to result from their activity and they are prone to cynicism and disillusionment when the changes are not forthcoming.

A third comparison can be found in the ivory-towered campuses of the universities where the debate of form vs. substance, and style vs. skill has raged for many years. The ambiguities of the debate continue and the people who have devoted their lives to making the universities intellectual oases have suffered many an identity crisis on the way.

One of the things which those in ministry have in common with the areas outlined above is the lack of an overall or general supporting theory for their work. In the rush to become relevant and in the haste to solve important social problems, they have embarked upon whole programs of social action, ministerial action, business programs and intellectual directions without giving very much thought to an underlying theory. For the minister the theory, by definition, should be theological in nature and it is perhaps their greatest lack that there is no theological basis for much of what they do. Without a strong theoretical base, activity loses direction and people quickly become bored and dissatisfied with the amount of energy that they are putting out vis à vis the returns that they are experiencing. They tend under these circumstances to criticize the people they are working with for their lack of interest, their lack of productive motivation, when, in fact, they probably ought to be looking much more at their own activity and the theoretical foundations which support it.

There is, it seems safe to say, little pride in the priesthood today. Although individual priests might be pleased with their own accomplishments (some justifiably, others due to smugness), there is little sense that across the board the priesthood is a highly respected profession. And it is extremely difficult to function in a positive manner, with few doubts about what you can accomplish, in the midst of an environment that seems mediocre at best. Discouragement among priests is an understandable malaise, given the state of the profession today.

This discouragement, along with the uncertainty about identity, is a significant factor in the lack of success of many ministerial teams in parishes today. Where ministerial teams are able to exercise a positive influence in the religious community, you invariably find a pastor who has managed to rise above the discouragement of many of his fellow priests. Father Bill Clark is of a generation of priests most of whom are very unhappy and discouraged with their role as pastor in suburban parishes around Chicago. These men find it impossible to lead a successful ministerial team. They worry about whether "it is fair" for the secretary to eat lunch in the rectory instead of providing the dynamic force for new activities—be they mens' discussion clubs or a speaker with a new idea to be invited for the community to hear—as Bill Clark does.

And it is inevitable that if the ministerial staff of a parish is not functioning well, the parish as a whole has little impact on the lives of the people. This fact is often lamented by people who have a very radical understanding of parish and who come out of an ecclesiology of gifts and who feel, even though the leadership of the parish cannot get along among themselves, the parish itself will in some way flower. This might be true in some ideal world but in practice unless the ministerial center is doing well with one another, the larger parish community which it serves flounders.

One reason ministerial teams fail to function effectively is that, lacking a sound theological basis and good leadership, they fall into a group therapy approach to community religious leadership. We reject this approach which is characterized by such disastrous terms as "parish team" and "staff meeting." In principle, surely, those who work together on any project should be free intermittently to meet and discuss their common goals. The parish staff meeting sounded like a good idea when it began fifteen years ago (more or less) and in many places it continues to be a good idea. Yet, in all too many situations, it would seem that it has become a psychoanalytic exercise in fixation, transference, counter-transference, and regression, and that the parish team, instead of being a means to an end (the service of the people in a local religious community), turns out to become an end in itself and the problems, internal and relational of the parish team, consume far more time and energy than do the problems of the parish. The parish teams have, in so many cases, turned into surrogate families, with all the unresolved conflicts, frustrations, aggressions, defenses, antagonisms, and need to punish which, unresolved in childhood family situations, are resurfacing, and invading if not destroying the work that is supposed to be going on in the parish community. To the question that often arises—ought decisions by the parish team be made by unanimity or by majority vote and does the priest have the right to veto the decisions of the parish teams—we respond by saying that once such questions have arisen the atmosphere in the local religious community has been so poisoned that there is very little that can be done and the attempt to impose theological or sociological solutions is bound to poison the atmosphere even more.

First of all, we propose to deal with the issue of leadership of a ministerial staff (which we take to be of enormous practical importance in many parishes) with three sound and indisputable adminstrative science propositions.

1) When someone assumes a position within a community in which he or she is going to exercise professional skills, that person ought to be given the maximum amount of independence and discretion on how the goals for which

she or he has been hired are to be achieved, and should be judged finally on performance in the achievement of these goals. That person ought to be given the maximum amount of support from other professionals working in the same community and not be subject to harrassment, either by the other professionals directly, or indirectly by the acquiescence of the other professionals in the criticisms and complaints of malcontents.

For example, a director of religious education has been hired by the parish and for the pastor or the other members of the team not to support that director of religious education is almost criminally irresponsible and is indeed another admission that the pastor or whoever was responsible for the hiring made a grave personnel mistake at the beginning. If the rights and freedoms of individuals are clearly violated or if the professional performance is clearly incompetent, that is another matter. But if you are not willing to give a colleague the maximum amount of freedom to exercise her or his responsibility, then you should not have hired the colleague in the first place.

2) Meetings should be kept at an absolute minimum and they should be rigorously limited to the professional tasks at hand. They should not become group therapy sessions or ideological conflict situations. If members of a team of professional colleagues have psychological problems, they should resolve them outside of the context of such meetings and hopefully outside of the context of the exercise of professional responsibility. If someone in the parish team needs psychotherapy, to put the matter more bluntly, let them seek the psychotherapy from a professional therapist and not at staff meetings. Similarly, whatever one's position may be on, for example, the ideological issues of feminism, these issues should simply be

kept out of the professional relationships among colleagues working in the local religious community. If consensus on the essential issues necessary for a colleague relationship turns into an arena for ideological conflicts or for personality regressions to childhood masquerading as ideological conflicts, then the relationship never should have begun in the first place. The sooner it is terminated the better.

3) There can be in any task-oriented working group only one principal leader. That leader, if he has any sense at all, presides over his colleagues with the sophisticated skill of a coalition builder, a consenus organizer, and a compromise constructer. He does not, to quote the New Testament, "lord it over others." He leads more by asking questions than by providing answers, though there are times when he also must, if anything is to be done at all, provide answers and make decisions. Consensual leadership, incidentally, is not merely virtuous behavior when one is dealing with a group of professionals. It is an organizational necessity. Putting it more bluntly, the parish priest, in dealing with his professional colleagues, must have all the subtle political and diplomatic skills of a precinct captain. He must be able to keep everybody happy, at least reasonably happy for a reasonable amount of time. If he cannot do that, he ought not to be a leader. If your particular leader cannot do those things, then find yourself another one, but do not waste time and money by trying to force him to be such a leader, nor abandon your responsibility to serve the people in a local religious community by trying to force a non-precinct captain professional leader into being one. Don't fight with him, in other words; get out.

We will not, in the present context, go into a long discussion of why there can be but one principal leader. We simply take it that most organizational and social scientist observers would confirm that dictum. By way of a shorthand argument, the principal leader need not sign all the checks himself or keep the books, but he is the one ultimately to see that the checks are signed and the books are kept.

There is, be it noted here, a very subtle difference between collective leadership and consensual leadership. In the former, agreement of all participating professionals is required for all major decisions and that agreement must normally be hammered out in time-consuming, agonizing meetings (which leave little time or energy to implement the decisions that have been reached). Consensual leadership requires, rather, that everybody knows what is happening, that the consent of the relevant professionals be obtained for any activity that infringes on their area of responsibility and competence, and that all the collaborating professionals be kept reasonably happy for a reasonable amount of the time. Collective leadership paralyzes any working group. Consensual leadership is absolutely essential for an effective working group.

The pastor who uses these administrative science positions is also attuned to the interaction between the members of the ministerial or professional groups in his community. The environment that ministers create among themselves and the quality and extent of their interaction with one another is crucial for their success in meeting the needs of the community. When a pastor is confident in his own professional role he is bound to exercise a positive influence on professionalism among other ministers in the community. He must, however, as part of his leadership function, be attuned to the various dimensions of the interaction that exists among the ministers in his parish.

We will briefly consider three dimensions of this interaction since the fostering of positive interaction will reinforce both the pastor's and the other minister's sense of professionalism (for more detailed analysis see John Shea, "Ministers Ministering to Ministers"). A pastor who understands the flow of interaction between all the members of the ministerial team (including himself) is better equipped to deal with questions of his own role in the community.

1) The range of interaction of members of a ministerial team are varied but move on a continuum from *primary group* through *community* to *association.* The primary group is a small, close-knit group where the range of interaction is extensive. The personal problems of any minister become the concern of the group. At the other end of the continuum, the association is a formal organization whose energies are directed outside themselves. The ministerial team then is strictly task oriented which seems contrary to the nature of ministry in the local church. The association model is usually rejected not only because it seems cold, but because it is deemed ineffective. The community approach to interaction, which combines some aspects of a primary group and some of an association seems the wisest. Here ministers deal with the personal-public areas of feelings and actions. The personal-private areas of ministers' lives are left for groups other than the ministerial team. At the same time a strictly public role defined interaction belongs to more impersonal groups.

2) Style of interaction on ministerial teams, as in all positive relationships, must consistently be both sup-

portive and challenging. If it is only supportive, it fails to perform the evaluating function necessary in any professional undertaking. If it is only challenging, it erodes effective relating and causes defensiveness. To combine support and challenge, ministers must have a foundation of self-respect, interpersonal skills and clarity of tasks. All team members must be comfortable and competent in their roles and they must respect each other's talents and achievements.

3) Content of interaction must include more than the immediate and practical concern with "getting things done!" The question of theological identity is crucial for all members of a ministerial team if they are to successfully grapple with the issues involved in their particular tasks. This is especially critical when there are differing theological views operating beneath the surface. Ministerial teams need to theologically reflect and explore their community identity and mission if they are to surface these differences and determine if they are irreconcilable or if they can creatively interact. This is especially critical as people from diverse backgrounds begin to function on ministerial teams.

The pastor who appreciates the importance of professionalism will find his own sense of identity, as well as that of others serving and ministering in the community, greatly enhanced when he is able to support a range, style and content of interaction among the ministers that is creative of good living and working for the ministers and for the larger religious community.

We conclude this section of our study of religious leadership in the local church with a call for disciplined skill and art in the priesthood. We maintain that an understanding of the role of the priest as religious leader of the local community is based on the need for the local community to have one person who functions as leader. This leadership, however, is not a leadership of "giving orders" but is one of obtaining consent from those who wish to be led. This view of leadership is rooted in principles of community leadership and in a theological understanding of the priest as representative of "Christ as Transformer." With this theoretical basis, priests should be able to develop standards regarding their role as encourager and challenger, as faith reflector and as mediator of the implications of a "Christ as Transformer" understanding of faith. The priest who "walks both sides of the street" will be one who has a true sense of who he is (no question marks for him), who has been supported through good seminary education and/or a program of continuing education and who has confidence in himself and in the possibilities of his profession. To help point the way for the development of an educational program for the kind of priestly leadership needed in a parish that works, we now turn to the concluding section of our study with its proposals for the direction of priestly education.

PART III

Resources and Training for the Priest-Leader

CHAPTER 13

Skills and Education

SOME people seem to be born leaders. Others acquire the skills of leadership through on-the-job training; they develop "street smarts" as they move through different situations. Still others have talents that have been nurtured through an educational process geared to turning out leaders. Given the right educational process, a person of average intelligence and talents can be helped to utilize these abilities in a way consistent with the tasks of his particular life. However, even the "born leader" must practice the same skills as the "made to order" leader; the former does it almost instinctively, the latter has learned his lesson well.

We suspect that Bill Clark is a combination of all three types of leaders. His natural tendencies toward openness and caring must have been aided by his ability to walk both sides of the street in Mary, Seat of Wisdom parish. Even though his formal seminary training did not prepare him for the kind of leadership needed in a modern suburban parish, his own continuing education program has kept him open to new ideas when many men his age have quit having constructive, creative thoughts. Though we do not know the particular process he went through to develop his style of leadership, we think his success as the motivating force in Mary, Seat of Wisdom parish qualifies him as an example of a priest who meets the standards of professionalism outlined in the previous chapters.

We are not suggesting that all priests and priests-in-training strive to become copies of Bill Clark. His particular style of leadership works well in a parish like Mary, Seat of Wisdom and is a reflection of his personality. Other equally successful pastoral leaders have different personalities and are working in different settings. For example, George Clements, pastor at Holy Angels, an inner city, black parish, and Leo Mahon at St. Victor's, a blue collar parish in Calumet City, are two other Chicago priests who qualify as excellent pastoral leaders. Yet the three men are quite different in the way they exercise leadership. What they have in common, and what we are suggesting all successful pastoral leaders must have, is the ability to gain the assent of the community to their leadership as well as the ability to utilize their leadership role in a professional manner. They are men who challenge, comfort, proclaim the transformative power of the Christian message, and initiate the process of faith reflection for both the other professional ministers in the parish and the laity. Anyone aspiring to a position of pastoral leadership should be able to do the same, no matter what his personality, his particular leadership style or the situation of the community he serves.

The training of the priest, both in the seminary before ordination and his in-service training while in the ministry, must be aimed primarily at developing sources and skills that will assist his growth as a professsional religious leader. We will now examine the particular skills needed for religious leadership in the local church.

When we consider the need for the religious leader to be a person who comforts and challenges we must begin by noting, first of all, that the religious leader is a religious leader, and that his comfort and challenge is not the same as that provided by a psychiatrist or a social worker or even a loving parent. He does not primarily deal with the personality disturbances which impede the successful functioning of the personality. Nor does he deal primarily with the community disorders that are the proper concern of the social worker or the community organizers. Nor does he provide the fundamental reassurance that is the responsibility of the parent. He may share in the skills of all other functionaries, and in some times and in some places he may have to assume their function by default. His primary mission is to comfort and challenge by "telling the stories." He must articulate and interpret the religious symbols in a language and manner appropriate for the particular circumstances in which he is exercising his mission of comfort and challenge to a given person or persons.

It, therefore, follows that at least three basic skills are required of a local community religious leader. He must, 1) know the story, 2) be able to tell the story and 3) be sensitive to which version of the story is appropriate to a given set of circumstances.

And, according to the reaction of the laity, most priests are deficient in all three of these tasks. The data from several NORC surveys which revealed attitudes of the Catholic laity towards the sermons and the pastoral skills of their clergy leave little doubt on the subject. Indeed, satisfaction with the level of professional performance of the clergy has gone down in the last decade and a half, despite the various innovations in ministry training. The "field work" and "clinical pastoral experience" have not prevented the erosion of lay satisfaction with clerical performance. Some argue that all these quasi psychiatric programs have actually been responsible for the decline in satisfaction with clerical performance.

The clinical pastoral approach in particular was absorbed from Protestant ministry training without any adaptation on the part of Catholic seminary leaders. Those who would use it without either substantive or, for the most part, doctrinal resources were, in effect, being trained to be "bargain basement" psychiatrists, because it was not clear that the clergy had any resources uniquely their own to offer. One has the impression that in much of the "practical" ministerial training given to Catholic seminarians the same assumption is present. One does not learn the stories either because the stories are not worth telling, or because it is not clear that telling them will have any effect, or because one can by no means be sure that those whose mission it is to tell the stories are ready to believe them themselves. Nor does one pay any attention to the liturgy which enacts the story because, if the stories are irrelevant, then surely the liturgy which re-presents them is also irrelevant.

In the perspective taken in this project, however, the stories are still relevant and the liturgies are still relevant, and while psychological skills are by no means useless and, indeed, can be very helpful, they are no substitute either for knowing the stories or being able to tell them.

We contend that the training for local religious leaders ought to be cognitive and rhetorical. They ought to be taught the best of the current Catholic theological knowledge and the best of the current rhetorical and expressive skills. They must, in short, be able to read and write. It is not at all clear that many of the clergy, young or old, are able to do either. To put the case at its bare minimum, the future clergy must be able to preach a good sermon. Such preaching requires the continual reading which is necessary to sustain the thought that must go into sermons and skillful writing which is required to compose the sermons. Anyone who thinks that good sermons are being preached by the Catholic clergy today has neither listened to the complaints of the laity, nor inspected the statistical evidence. If a good sermon is evidence that a priest can read and write, then one must say that, regrettably, most priests are functional illiterates.

We have the impression that there is a pervasive anti-intellectualism both in the administration and the faculty and in the student body of most Catholic seminaries. Ideas and knowledge are not important, nor are the skills of understanding and literate self-expression. Sincerity, conviction and sympathy (often of the most shallow sort) are thought to be the requirements for successful ministry. Even the homiletic courses which directly pertain to the Sunday sermon—the most important and most effective means available to the clergyman according to the empirical evidence, are poorly taught and generate only minimal interest. The development of the background knowledge necessary for sermon preparation and the background skills for intelligent and communicative writing are not thought to be that important. The need for such skills is something that is not even a matter for discussion.

It may be argued that the courses *de deo uno et trino* and *de verbo incarnato* as they were traditionally taught in the seminary may not have been especially relevant for local parish ministry. However, at the present time there are more than enough resources available to the theology instructor and the theology student to provide the solid intellectual and cognitive grounding and theological and scriptural resources that would be essential to adequate Sunday preaching and to adequate performances of the other comforting and/or challenging ministerial situations in which the priest will find himself.

To put the matter simply and bluntly: no one ought to be ordained who is not well informed about both the Catholic theological tradition and its contemporary restatement and especially about the breakthroughs of modern exegesis. Furthermore, no one ought to be ordained who is not willing to solemnly commit himself to continue his education in these matters. It is not enough for a priest to be "nice" to people (much less a "nice guy"). It is necessary for him to be nice religiously, which means to speak with knowledge and understanding, with depth and conviction on religious matters.

He must also be able to translate religion into the everyday language that men and women understand. He must, therefore, not only be able to read. He also must be able to write. Matters of homiletic style—gestures, voice, tone, etc.—are not unimportant. But they are surely second to the acquisition to the elementary abilities of English composition. Elegance of style is admirable, though for most people it can only be acquired through long practice. But there is no excuse for anyone whose principal job is to communicate to be unable to express himself clearly, concisely and intelligently. Since few of us are born with that ability, it means that constant practice in composition is required through the seminary years. The priest-to-be and the ordained priest must have facility in systematic and intelligible self-expression. He is, after all, competing with

Harry Reasoner and John Chancellor, and the standards for clarity of communication maintained by such communicators are the ones by which the priest will be judged by his people.

It ought not to be necessary in this book to repeat the classic theory of liberal education: one learns how to read and to write and to think in the ordinary course of events by being exposed to the classics of literature, and by being forced to think and to communicate comprehensibly about the issues raised in such classics. Literary style can rarely be acquired by direct pursuit. It is, rather, the result of being forced to think and to articulate one's thoughts about "great ideas" and their "classic" expression.

If the choice, then, is clinical pastoral experience, or Shakespeare, one must come down unequivocally on the side of Shakespeare (though there is no reason why practical experience and liberal education cannot be combined).

Religious and theological knowledge and clarity of thought and expression are no substitutes for the third requirement—sensitive sympathy to the time, the place and the person with whom one is dealing. It seems problematic that such skills can be taught, either in traditional classrooms or by modern psychological "encounter" techniques. One learns through the development of tenderness and affection. The skill is analagous to the experienced professional quarterback who can "read" the other team's defensive alignment in a fraction of a second with one quick glance. The best way currently available to us to facilitate the development of this skill is found in the "faith reflection" technique that combines 1) listening skills, 2) theological skills, and 3) change agent skills. These can be developed through a combination of understanding the theory behind the practice of these skills and the actual practice of them both during the period of seminary training and on-the-job both before and after ordination. One is never completely competent in any of these areas. Rather the pastoral leader who is successful is continually updating his techniques in acquiring more expertise and in putting it into practice in all three of these areas. Such a pastor is practicing the art of pastoral theology.

Briefly, the methodology of pastoral theology requires that the pastor have listening skills that allow him to identify and elaborate the central, paradigmatic experience of the people with whom he is working; that he know his territory with a certain objectivity so he knows what is going on even before many of the people know it themselves. He is the trailblazer who recognizes needs and concerns and is able to articulate them, even when the people who are experiencing them have not become conscious of their existence. He is able to spot these problems, oftentimes, because he has kept abreast of research in social science areas that are relevant for his community.

For example, in a parish composed largely of middle-aged adults he recognizes the stress caused by the demands that many of the parishioners are feeling from both their teenage children and their aging parents. Or he is aware of the particular stress the women in his community are experiencing as they approach the empty nest stage, not because he has read that all women are eager to jump on the women's liberation bandwagon or, conversely, are adamently against ERA, but because he is aware of what women in the particular socio-economic situation of his parishioners are said to be feeling and he is alert for signs of how this experience is manifesting itself in the lives of the women in his community.

To be a successful listener the pastor must belong to this community. He must walk the streets of the community in both a literal and figurative way while maintaining a stance somewhere between absorption and aloofness. If he loses himself in the community, he becomes incapable of ministering to it and becomes "one of the guys," unable to challenge. If he remains aloof from the everyday life of the community, he will be incapable of comforting when comfort is an opening to faith reflection. He must develop the skill of empathetic listening. And he must be prepared to make mistakes. Successful listening takes time, patience and practice, and sometimes even the most expert listener misreads the signals. The best indicator of the validity of an observation based on effective listening is the "head nodding" that occurs in the community when it is made.

Identifying paradigmatic experiences in the community is only the first step. Listening skills must be reinforced by theological skills. The man who is responsible for initiating faith reflection in a community must be wise in the ways of the Christian tradition. As we observed previously in this chapter, he must have a superb theological education. He must know the stories of our faith. He must love the bible. And he must be willing to continually update his understandings of the visions and values present in the tradition. When he has a solid background in theological skills, he finds the vision and values jumping out at him when he uncovers paradigmatic experiences in the life of the community. He doesn't have to embark on a long search for something in the faith that might apply to a situation.

The pastor, who, through the practice of his listening skills, recognizes a paradigmatic experience in the community and uses his theological skills to ascertain visions and values in the tradition that speak to that experience, gives the experience a Christian perspective. In most instances this perspective then requires the practice of change-agent skills to relate faith to action. The visions and values of the tradition give hints about possible responses to a particular situation, but there is no one response that is fitting for every instance of the situation. There are implications for life-style and strategies of actions inherent in a Christian perspective, but there is no prescription for exact behavior. Learning to articulate the Christian perspective in such a way that its implication for the life of the community are apparent requires change-agent skills. Comfort and challenge, not order-giving, are essential for any community that is seeking to develop a life-style congruent with the Christian perspective.

The married couple who are in a rut in their relationship need the warm images of the Christian tradition articulated in such a way that they recognize the challenge to grow in their sexual relationship as a means of discovering God already present in their lives. The pastor who is challenging them to initiate a change in their life must be prepared to assist them through the process of death and resurrection which must take place if they are to appreciate the Christian perspective in their relationship. He must be skilled in understanding the process of change and the effects this will have on people's lives. He must understand how he and the entire ministerial staff of the parish can support married couples as they attempt to implement behavior suggested by the Christian perspective. He must be available with the message of "forgiveness" for those who experience difficulty in the process of change. An understanding of his role as agent of change as well as the entire process of change is essential if faith reflection is to encourage the process of religious encounter to its final step of implications for the lives of those who have an experience of mystery.

In conclusion, we find that the professional pastoral leader must be a multi-talented individual, with background and skills in many areas. Above all, however, he must be a *religious* leader. To be this religious leader he needs the skills of the religious reflector enriched by his ability to proclaim the stories of the people and the stories of the tradition in an articulate way. He must be competent as a preacher as well as being competent as a listener and an agent of change. And he must be committed to a lifelong learning process. Only then will he be equipped to lead the members of a local religious community in this contemporary world.

There is no one model of how a pastor practices all of these skills, just as there is no one way of acquiring them. Bill Clark, George Clements and Leo Mahon are examples of how they can be acquired in spite of a seminary experience not conducive to obtaining these skills. But they also point the way for the modern seminary administrator who is developing programs for priests-in-training as well as continuing education for priests already ordained. We must now turn our attention to some specifics of how these skills enrich the task of pastoral leadership as well as what learning programs would contribute to the development of these skills.

CHAPTER 14

The Development of the Religious Imagination of the Religious Leader

MANY priests and also many priests-in-training see little relevance between seminary training and the experience of the real world of pastoral leadership. This is understandable in view of the seminary systems of the pre-Vatican II world of the Catholic Church. Unfortunately it continues to be true of most of the seminary systems that are presently claiming to be relevant. In both instances those responsible for designing curriculum for the priests-in-training were not cognizant of the interaction between religion and the creative imagination. They failed to appreciate the fact that religion (as the individual's experience of mystery) has its origin in the creative imagination. Any seminary training that would hope to develop priests who will be *religious* leaders needs to develop programs that respond to this phenomenon. With this in mind we will now consider the role of creative imagination in the training of priests.

Our thesis is that a highly developed creative imagination is essential in the ministry of the priest. We will use sociological theory and research evidence to sustain this thesis, though it is congruent with both Bernard Lonergan's notion of "perception" and Alfred North Whitehead's conception of "prehension." Both philosophers hold that "out of the corner of our eye," so to speak, in the act of knowing we perceive purpose, design, even love binding together the cosmos. We contend that the "out of the corner of the eye" aspect of knowing is precisely where religion finds its origin and power, and that, therefore, religion is primarily an activity of the creative imagination. The priest, therefore, must be skilled in both resonating to his own creative imagination and stirring up resonances in the creative imaginations of others.

There are a number of different names for that dimension of the human personality which we call the creative imagination—a word taken from the psychoanalyst Leonard Kubie, who also calls it the preconscious—an aspect of the self somewhere between the unperceived unconscious and the fully perceived conscious.

Jacques Maritain, in words similar to Kubie's, calls it the "creative intuition" and compares it to Thomas Aquinas's agent intellect (*intellectua agens,* if you prefer the mother tongue). Others would call it the poetic intuition or the poetic faculty. St. Paul seems to refer to the same dimensions of the person when he says that the Spirit speaks to our spirit, to, it would seem from the context, the spontaneous, creative, fine edge of the soul.

By whatever name, this dimension of the personality may be conceived (or, perhaps, imagined) as a radar screen on which are scanned, in endlessly shifting arrangements, the images which have been drawn by the senses out of the world experience. In this scanning process, images are juxtaposed in constantly changing constellations which are inchoate poems and stories, metaphors and narratives which combine various elements in our experience, past and present. The creative imagination edits and compares, connects and separates, simplifies and distorts, convolutes and modifies; it performs these activities some-times "mindlessly" in the strict sense that the mind is not attending, and at other times with deliberate purpose in that the mind is carefully listening, searching for insight and understanding.

It seems not unreasonable to link the creative imagination with the right lobe of the brain and to consider the times when it is given the full freedom to operate an altered state of consciousness. At such times (which can, of course, be deliberately induced by one means or another) one can literally hear the stories and poems which are being created, so much so that the Greek myth of the Muse, the outside inspiring agent, takes on a certain amount of plausibility. It is worth noting, by the way, that in certain kinds of scientific analysis (including sociologi-cal work with a conversational computer system) this "preconscious" dimension also operates. (Here the work of the philosopher Michael Polynni seems to parallel our thesis.)

We contend that it is precisely in this creative imagina-tion where religion has its origin and power and that, the priest with a poorly developed creative imagination will be so devoid of religious sensibility as to be ineffective as a priest.

It is necessary here to make two precisions so our argu-ment will not be misunderstood.

1) We are not excluding from religion the importance of discursive intellect or rational reflection. On the contrary, because we are reflecting creatures we must be able to go beyond story and poem, beyond picture and song to artic-ulate propositions and eventually to philosophical re-ligion. Creeds, catechisms and *Summae* are utterly essen-tial to the human condition. Because religion begins in the

imagination does not mean that it should end there, but merely that we ought not to forget the fact that it does, indeed, begin there. Among certain right wing Catholics now there is a contempt for "religious experience," as though it was utterly irrelevant to the human condition and to human faith. Perhaps there is some merit in their contempt because much of what passes for religious experience today in the Church is both shallow and unreflective. It is not of such experiences that we are speaking.

2) Nor of either religious experience or the religious imagination in which the stories and pictures of the experience resonate and remain pure "emotion." Quite the contrary, the religious imagination is an aspect of the personality of an intellectual creature and is both affected by that creature's intellectual development and operates as a dimension of intellect. The conscious mind is not absent from the creative imagination, not ever; and it is especially present when it pauses to listen in the altered state of consciousness called the creative process. Indeed, the term "preconscious intellect" is in our judgment the perfect description of the dimension we are describing—so, too, is Thomas's "Agent," or if you will, "Active Intellect."

We will not enter into a dispute as to whether the development of conscious intellect or the development of the creative imagination is important for the work of the priest, though it is our impression that neither is taken very seriously these days. Both are important, indeed. Both are indispensable and that seems to be enough.

However, one must say that if sermons are terrible—and the judgment of the laity is that they are indeed terrible—the problem may be more in the lack of creative imagination in the priest that in the lack of cognitive knowledge.

We now turn to the sociological theory which supports our thesis. We will describe this theory under eight headings.

1) *Human nature has a built-in propensity to hope.* Whether that hope is genetically programmed, as Lionel Tiger has argued, or merely a powerful psychological need is not pertinent for our theory. It is sufficient to say that in our research more than four-fifths of the American people gave hopeful or optimistic responses to potentially tragic situations. Death research, resuscitation research, dream analysis all demonstrate this powerful and persistent tendency of humans to hope even when the situation seems hopeless, even when they can find no specific content to their hope.

2) *Humans also have the capacity for experiences which renew their hope.* These experiences may, for some people, be the spectacular experience of which William James wrote in his *Varieties of Religious Experience.* These experiences may also be much less spectacular—a desert sunset, a touch of a friendly hand, a reconciliation after a quarrel, the grin on the face of a toddler, solving an ethical or mathematical problem, even a good night's sleep. Experiences like this, are experiences of "gratuity," nice things that did not have to happen, but did. We encounter with them the limitations of our existence which also confirm that despite those limitations, our existence is "gifted," something that did not have to happen, did not have to be, yet is. Such experiences occur with varying degrees of intensity in virtually everyone's life, providing hints of purpose, "rumors of angels," intimations of something, encounters with "otherness."

Creatures born with the propensity to hope, we are confirmed in that propensity by certain "encounters" in our lives. That which is "encountered" is experienced most often simply as "otherness"; but, on occasion, or frequently for some people, it can be a powerful, demanding, passionately loving "otherness." Hence, on reflection, we speak of the "otherness" as "The Other." Both historically and psychologically we believe this to be the origin of first the image, and then the concept of, "God."

Philosophically, an examination of religion may well begin with the question of whether God exists.[1] But, humanly, the experience of gratuity and the encounter with The Other precede the question of whether God exists. (Though most of us, of course, come to our limit-experience with an existing notion of God, a notion which may or may not fit that which we experience.) However, both the God concept and the God issues are derivative. The more fundamental and primordial question is whether reality is such as to guarantee the propensity to hope. Perhaps even more basic: is reality truly that which we experience in our interludes of hopefulness? John MacQuarrie, an English theologian, put the question nicely when he said that the primary question is whether reality (or Reality) is gracious (or Gracious). From the point of view of the social scientist approaching religion, the basic question is "What are the stories that reveal reality as gracious?" "What impact do such stories have on a person's life?"

3) While any reality may trigger a "grace" experience (and, hence, everything is sacramental in the sense that everything has the potentiality of revealing the source of our hopefulness), *there are certain realities which because of their power, their importance, or their relevance are*

233

especially likely to trigger such experiences (hence, are sacraments par excellence): fire, the sun, water, the moon, oil, love, sex, marriage, birth, death, community. For reasons of biology, psychology, or culture, these realities seem especially likely to trigger grace experiences for many human beings.

For example, the Jewish Passover recapitulates three different preSinai pagan spring festivals, all resonating with the fertility of spring: the unleavened bread festival of an agricultural people, the paschal lamb festival of a pastoral people, and the fire and water festival of the more sophisticated urban people. The Christian passover absorbed these powerful and ancient symbols and articulated more sharply the fire and water symbolism by absorbing a more explicit intercourse rite, plunging the fiery candle (the male organ) into the life-giving water (the female organ), which originated in Roman fertility rites. We can leave to psychologists and historians of religion explanations of both the power and persistence of such symbolism. Here it need only be noted that they stir up deep resonances in the human imagination.

4) *The experience is recorded, first of all, in that aspect of the personality we normally call "the imagination."* The experience of grace, initially, is an impact on the senses and then is filtered through the imagination where it has an enormous and sometimes overwhelming effect. Even long after the experience is over, the residue remains in the imagination, capable of recollection and of exciting once again resonances of the experience. The interaction between experience and imagination is complex and intricate. From the repertory of images and pictures available to any given person's or community's imagina-

tion, the individual or community will respond to the experience and shape both the perception and the recollection of the experience, if not the experience itself. Thus, the apostles' Easter experience of Jesus as not dead, but alive, was encoded in the imagery of contemporary Judaism. Jesus as Moses, Jesus as Adam, Jesus as prophet, as Messiah, even as "resurrected" in accordance with the "story" common in Pharasaic Judaism—all these images or "stories" were part of the imaginative repertory available to the followers of Jesus. Their experience of Jesus perceived as alive triggered such images and pictures. The images and pictures shaped the experience, or, at least, their resonance to it. In the process, the images, pictures, and stories were themselves transformed so that they meant something rather different to the apostles afterwards, when they tried to describe the experience. Jesus was "like" a new Adam, and yet there was more to be said because the Adam "story" had been changed as a result of the Easter experience.

We cite this classic, tradition-shaped grace experience because it provides such a clear example of the subtle interaction between imagination and experience. Presumably, interactions of that sort occur in many, if not all experiences of grace, although until we have much more research on the psychology of the experience itself, no one will be able to chart the precise process with any degree of confidence.

5) *The purpose of religious discourse, at least of the most elementary variety, is not to communicate doctrinal propositions, but to stir up in the other person resonances of experiences similar to that which the religious storyteller himself or herself has had.* Thus, the telling each year in

Holy Week of the story of the death and resurrection of Jesus, complete with all the profoundly resonating liturgical imagery, is not designed primarily to communicate doctrinal propositions, but to rekindle memories of death-rebirth experiences that have marked the lives of the hearers and to link those resonances to the historic experience of Christians through the ages, leading back to the founding experience itself. The Easter story is primarily designed to rekindle memories of grace experiences and link them with overarching memories in the historical tradition. Religion as story leaps from imagination to imagination, and only then, if at all, from intellect to intellect.

6) *Religion becomes a communal event when we are able to link our own grace experience with the overarching experience of this religious tradition* (or a religious tradition), that is to say, when we perceive a link between our experience of grace and the tradition's experience of grace, when we become aware that there is a correspondence or a correlation between the resonating picture or story in our imagination and our story passed on by our religious heritage. At that point the experience of grace is a private event, or at least one which is not perceived as linked to anything that is formally known as religion. (In our subsequent discussion of the film, *All That Jazz,* we will illustrate how a profound grace experience need not be perceived at all as formally religious.) However, it is worth noting that most of us are products of religious heritages, and there is a powerful tendency in most of our personalities to resonate our experiences in and through the images that we inherited from our tradition. Our own experiences of grace give an inchoate meaning to the story of our lives, they hint at purposes which exist beyond our-

236

selves, they suggest that the story of our life, which has a beginning, a middle, and a trajectory toward conclusion, may well have a gracious purpose. Articulated with, and resonating together with, stories of religious heritage, these religious stories constitute a fundamental theme, a basic *leit motif* which underpins and validates our own existence. They have now become a set of "unique" symbols to which Geertz refers in his definition of religion.

We are all storytellers, playing the leading role in the story that is our own life. Even if some philosophers insist that our life is a series of random events, we perceive life events lived through a number of basic themes within the context of beginning, middle, and thrust toward conclusion. One of the basic themes is religious or ultimate; it is the theme, or if you will, the subplot, of the play of our lives which gives it final meaning by linking it, on the one hand, to our own experiences of grace and, on the other hand, to the overarching story themes of our religious heritage.

7) *Just as much of the story of anyone's life is a story of relationship, so each person's religious story is a story of relationships.* (We walked the hills of Galilee and Jerusalem with him and knew he was special, but did not know just how special he was.) The principal sacraments in our lives are other human beings or, more precisely, our relationships with other human beings. While nonhuman objects, such as fire, water, sunset and mountain, may stir up experiences of grace, loving goodness is mostly perceived through relationships with other humans. We are, in other words, the principal sacrament, the principal sign, the principal symbol through which other persons encounter grace—experience hope validated—just as they

are the principal sacraments, the confirming grace and validating hope for us. Ultimate loving goodness, if it does, indeed, reveal itself, seems to reveal itself mostly through loving goodness.

8) *Thus, while religious teaching must certainly deal with ideas and in cognitive propositions, it must also stir up imaginative resonances and use stories and images.* Teachers must be story-tellers and poets so they can describe the experiences of loving goodness which are part of their life and their religious heritage in such a way that resonances of parallel experiences in the stories of the lives of those who are listening to them are excited. The loving goodness in their own lives must be linked to the Loving Goodness of the heritage and these linked stories of goodness—linked symbols, if you will—are then able to illumine the ambiguity and the uncertainties in the life of the listener as to the trajectory of their own personal stories. They are then free to permit their own narratives to be shaped by the theme of the overarching narrative. Such an exercise requires a considerable degree of skill in the art and the craft of expressing the creative imagination.

We now turn to empirical evidence which tends to support our theory of the creative imagination.

1) In our study of young adults, carried out with the generous assistance of the Knights of Columbus, we discovered that images of God as mother and lover, Mary and Jesus as warm, patient, kind and sympathetic, and heaven as an action-filled paradise of pleasures and delights could be combined into a scale which was a far more powerful predictor of religious behavior than propositional orthodoxy. Our so-called "grace-scale" correlated positively with de-

votion, thought of a religious vocation, commitment to social and racial justice, hopeful response to tragedy, and even sexual fulfillment in marriage at a level many times more powerful than the doctrinal orthodoxy scale—the latter, indeed, rarely produced any statistically significant relationships. Your "story of God" was a much more powerful influence on your religious behavior and your secular behavior than what you think about hell, papal authority and papal infallibility.

The methodology and the detailed findings of our research are beyond the scope of the present project. You may wish to consult, for example, *The Young Catholic Family* or *The Religious Imagination* for detailed proof. It suffices to say that there can be no doubt about the power of the religious imagination in human life.

2) Furthermore, the religious imagination is shaped primarily by relational experiences of loving goodness—with one's parents, with nature, directly with God, with school teachers, with friends, with parish priest and community, and with spouse. Indeed, the longer the marriage has endured and the more sexually fulfilling it is, the more powerful the mutual influences of husband and wife on each other's "story of grace." More than half of the variance in the grace scale can be accounted for by these relationships—a very powerful finding in social research.

Note that it is the quality of the relationship which matters. There is no correlation at all between years of Catholic education, years of CCD or, indeed, years of education, on the one hand, and the grace scale on the other. However, the young person's rating of the quality of religious instruction has a very strong effect on the shaping of the religious imagination, both directly and indirectly in the enhancement of the impact of subsequent forces such as spouse and current parish community.

3) The most notable effect of the parish community on both the religious imagination and on virtually everything else in the lives of young adults is the quality of preaching in the parish. Everything else in parish life and, indeed, in church life is unimportant compared to the quality of preaching. All the "media" issues—birth control, divorce, abortion, authority, the ordination of women—account for one-fourth as much of the variances in church identification as does Sunday preaching. Moreover, the impact of preaching on identification seems to be mediated by the religious imagination. Good sermons enhance the religious imagination of young people—make their imaginations more graceful—and, thus, incline them to be more likely to identify with the church. Alas, only ten percent of the young people think that the Sunday preaching is excellent. That which is the most important thing priests do, they do badly. And they seem to do it badly precisely because they cannot stir up stories of grace in the religious imagination of our congregations.

4) The Mary image is especially strong in the religious imagination of young Catholics. It encodes a benign experience of maternity in childhood and relates to a benign (sexuality fulfilling) experience of potential maternity or relation to a potential mother in adult life. The Mary image survives despite the fact that May crownings and rosary devotions no longer take place, despite the fact that young people no longer can sing "Bring Flowers of the Rarest," and despite the almost total absence of sermons and instructions about Mary precisely because young peo-

ple hear stories of Mary from their mothers and at Christmas time. The Mary Myth will survive no matter how much it is smothered by one kind of propositional religion and ignored by another kind of propositional religion because little kids will always see Crib scenes and because their mothers will always tell them that the Lady in the scene is God's mommy. For the child's religious imagination it is but a short jump, then, to think of God as mommy (and we can establish that correlation too). At a somewhat more sophisticated level the possibility that God loves us with the tender care, the sensitive passion and the fierce protectiveness of a mother with a young child has such rich imaginative resonances and such enormous power to rekindle hope. It is so appealing that it is unthinkable that the charm and the energy of the Mary imagery will ever be lost, no matter how desicated formal religious instruction might become.

The persistence and the impact of the Mary image proves that despite the invention of the printing press and the spread of literacy, religious heritages are still transmitted to young people the way they have always been—through story and picture. We are fond of looking back somewhat patronizingly at those illiterate ages which did not have schools and text books as being only semi-civilized religiously. Yet, it would seem that the basic power of religious socialization is still where it always was—in the story and the picture described by the parent and the parish priest. Schools are important, of course, and do represent net gain, so long as they do not snuff out the imagination. But, they are an adjunct to the traditional forms of religious socialization and not a substitute for them. More precisely, the combination of formal instruction and informal imagination ought to be the goal of all Catholic teaching so that both can reinforce one another. Again, the data sustain the importance of this combination.

What are the qualities of the effective poet/story teller/preacher? We take it that at least four characteristics are essential.[2]

1) He must be able to listen to his own muse, to hear the voices coming up from his own religious imagination, to perceive the stories of grace which are surging in his creative intuition.

2) He must also be able to listen to the stories of others so as to understand their "trajectories" and to sense their resonances.

3) Finally, he must be able to tell stories which link his imagination to the imaginations of others (while, at the same time, of course, teaching cognitive propositions).

4) He must be familiar with the stories of the Catholic religious heritage, not, indeed, as mechanical "tests" of faith or doctrines which must be believed "under pain of mortal sin," but as "mysteries," "sacraments," revelations of grace.

We would suggest that all four of these characteristics require considerable skill and self discipline. We all are born with both poetic and narrative ability. We have to learn both to speak prose and write nonfiction. Little kids juxtapose pictures and tell stories. Nonetheless, the raw, native creative imagination (and its ability, doubtless, varies with individuals, but all of us have enough of it) needs focus, practice, craft if it is to successfully stir up matching resonances in others.

One must be skilled at listening, at linking, at describing to be a good story teller. Cute little stories appended to a sermon after it has been prepared (if it is prepared) just won't do. In the absence of a rich, fully developed and carefully disciplined creative imagination the story will do more harm than good.

How, then, does the priest or the future priest go about developing his poetic faculty? Poetry? Someone has to be kidding. Perhaps, no one will say, as did a seminary teacher in the 1950's, that fiction is a waste of time. But, surely poetry and fiction are at best entertainment, relaxation, not part of the development of the effective preacher?

To which we would reply with a shorthand version of our thesis: The reason why priests get such rotten ratings as preachers is precisely because they are so devoid of the skills of imaginative communication, precisely because their creative imagination has become a vestigial organ, precisely because they are illiterate in the art and craft of poetry and story.

How, practically, can the development of the creative imagination be fostered? We are not pedagogues and can only make suggestions, leaving to others skilled in curriculum development how these suggestions might be implemented in the seminary.

1) Hermaneutics, which we take to be the craft of symbol interpretation, must be at the core of scripture studies. This means that the priest or priest-to-be must learn to look at the picture and the imagery of the scriptural texts and not merely at their cognitive meaning or their capacity to prove a doctrine which was articulated anywhere from five to twenty centuries after the text was written. We refer

you here to both Paul Ricoeur's theory of the meaning "in front of the text" and to Shea's current work on interpretation.

2) History of religions, a field which we think scarcely exists in seminaries, ought to be studied so that the priest will have some sense of the use of symbols and stories in other religious heritages and both their similarity and their diversity with the Christian stories. One knows one's own stories best when one can compare them with other stories.

3) There must be built-in opportunities and, indeed, requirements for self-expression—disciplined and practiced self-expression, not self-indulgence—in the training process. There must, also, be opportunities for creative feedback from peers and skilled teachers. Does this mean workshops in "creative writing" for the priest-to-be and the priest? How it is to be done is for others to decide, but the quality of preaching is so bad that we think the Church ought to be ready to try anything. Are we saying that priests ought to learn to write poetry and fiction? You better believe it!

4) Finally, there is no substitute in developing the imaginative faculty for contact with the great imaginations. When people hear this, they often ask for a reading list. We confess to being mind-boggled at such a request. Have they not heard of Shakespeare and Dante, Hopkins and Thompson, Chesterton and Belloc? Are the names of Bloy, Greene, Mauriac, Bernnanos, Powers, O'Connor, Joyce, Yates, Sienkiwicz, Manzoni, unknown?

We do not wait for the answers to those questions since we fear what they might be. Once there was a Catholic literary revival. Then, that was ridiculed. We should not concentrate, it was said, only on Catholic writers. We should read everyone. Instead, we read no one.

In addition to discovering our own imaginative heritage (try Henry Adams on the Virgin of Chartres, for example) we ought to pay attention to the works of our own times. Again, must one mention such obvious poets as Roethke and Berryman, Stevens and Lowel, Elliot and Berrigan? Or such novelists as Faulkner and Hemingway, and, heaven, help us, Saul Bellow and E. L. Doctorow?

But, in addition to the fact that familiarity with great works of the imagination is part of being an educated human being, our thesis is that they are a useful and probably indispensable challenge to the development of our creative imaginations. They are not either a luxury or an option to the development of the refined and disciplined creative imagination, to the training of the effective Sunday preacher.

Again to say that is to laugh. The temper of the American seminary and presbyteriate is such that the manhood of anyone making such an assertion is in doubt. That doesn't make the assertion wrong, however.

To conclude and summarize we will cite a grace experience that is both utterly secular and profoundly religious which has been shared with an enormous number of Americans by the choreographer and motion picture director, Bob Fosse. His encounter with grace was a death, or, more precisely a near-death experience which obviously had a shattering impact on his imagination. It would appear that in trying to make sense of the experience and the ecstatic joy which seemed to have come at the very point of his death, Fosse turned to the early literature on death and dying by Elizabeth Kubler-Ross and found that her description of the phases that preceded death (denial, anger, bargaining, resurrection and hope) corresponded to what happened to him. The five phases structured the dazzling, appalling, frightening and exhilarating film, *All That Jazz,* in which Fosse's imagination, working frantically and feverishly (with remarkable artistic skills, be it noted) tries to share with us his experience of grace at the turning point of life by calling forth memories, resonances of experiences we have had. If the framework of the movie is Kubler-Ross's phases, the story line is what Catholics used to call "the particular judgment," in which Fosse reviews his life with the Angel of Death and, while there is yet time, expresses sorrow, contrition and atonement. If he survives, he will at least try to do better. Then, in the final phase, at the end, Fosse participates in his own "farewell" television show in which "all that Jazz," which is his life, is scathingly reviewed. At the end, to the applause of all the characters that have been part of his life, Fosse trips up the stairs, out of the TV studio and runs down the long corridor toward the light. Waiting for him there is "Angelique," the Angel of Death, dressed in filmy bridal clothes, smiling warmly as she welcomes Fosse/Gideon into their nuptial chamber.

All That Jazz is a spectacular "religious story" of a spectacular experience of grace, told by a man with relentless, resourceful and extraordinary creative imagination. *All That Jazz* is a paradigm of our theory of the religious imagination. It shows a gratuitous experience of goodness, which renews hope, which creates a powerful impact on the imagination, leaves resonances which linger long after, and almost demands to be shared with others not by teaching them doctrinal propositions, but by telling them stories that resonate in their own imagination.

Furthermore, it is a story (R rating or not) of the fair bride, a messenger of hope and grace who waits at the end of the tunnel to convert death into life.

Pastoral leaders should be exposed to an educational process that will allow them to be faith reflectors for their communities in much the same way that Fosse attempts to share with us an experience of grace. Education geared to development of the creative imagination will enhance the religious leadership ability of those presently in ministry as well as those aspiring to it. Without the development of the creative imagination seminaries will continue to offer programs that neglect the *religious* aspects of pastoral leadership.

PART FOUR

Conclusion

CHAPTER 15

Policies, Recommendations and Suggestions

WE conclude this multiperson, multidisciplinary report with a number of statements, which will serve as both summaries and recommendations, to the various constituencies at which the report is aimed.

To Present and Future Parish Priests

1) There are few objective grounds either in the theological or the social sciences for the identity crisis which presently torments you. We do not deny the reality of either the crisis or the torment and do not seek to minimze the difficulties under which local religious leadership must currently labor. Our point, rather, is that there are resources available to transcend the present questions of identity. You may very well feel cheated by the fact that neither your theologians nor your episcopal leaders have yet provided you with these resources. In fact, for the time being, you may have to dig them out yourself. Nonetheless you are not without enormous resources and in time these resources will lead to the dawn of a new era of local community religious leadership.

2) The rise of the lay ministries—however they may be defined—does not make the priest less important. On the

contrary, the new ministries increase the demand for the coordinating-through-comfort-and-challenge style of leadership which is at the core of the priestly role.

3) The Sunday homily is one of the most important things you do. You must prepare for it both directly in the efforts that go into it each week and indirectly by developing your creative imagination so that you are skilled at telling the stories of God and the stories of Faith which are the essence of Catholic Christianity. The priest who preaches a good homily will be forgiven many other leadership faults.

4) The precinct captain model recommended in this book has skills essential for the work of comforting and challenging. No one can be expected to be born with such skills. They are acquired thru practice and mistakes—and never by the faint hearted or the cautious. To grow at these skills requires constant supportive feedback from your colleagues and your people. You must build such feedback into your life.

5) You must value the American form of local religious community which, as we have said, is absolutely unique in all the world. All too frequently in the last three decades we Americans have looked to other models—the city parishes of Paris, the worker priests of Mission France, the *Communitas de basso* of Latin America—as though they were the answers to American problems. While it is doubtless the case that we can learn much from the local communities of every corner of the Catholic world (and they from us, as far as that goes), we have often envied other nations their "new" religious forms without giving so much as the slightest thought that there is something posi-

tive to be said about the neighborhood/parish which grew up in the ethnic immigrant experience in this country. Yet, in fact, it is a highly successful innovation in church structure. It ought to be understood and valued in its own right. More to the point, perhaps, it is where we are. Even if one does not wish to celebrate the neighborhood parish—as the five of us do—one must at least concede that it is what we have. You will not go beyond it unless you understand it and value what is good about it. This will require that you leave aside, at least for the moment, any attempt to graft foreign growths on it and study both the theology and the social science of the American local religious community.

6) You must therefore require from your own leadership both a much more highly developed theory—based on the theological and human disciplines—of the American parish and the kind of in-service training which will help you to develop the skills of comfort and challenge which are required as you play your question-asking, precinct captain-listening, story telling role.

To Catholic Scholars and Funding Agencies

1) We urge Catholic theological scholars to develop programs of scholarly reflection based on the experience of the local religious community in the United States. Such reflection is a duty owed both to the rest of the Catholic world and to American Catholicism. Such groups as the Catholic Theological Society of America should establish committees and present reports on the local religious community which take into account both the historical and sociological evidence available on the American experience as well as the personal reflections of those currently

part of American parish life. It may well be necessary to overcome some characteristic American self-hatred to engage in such reflection—but it seems to us that the theological community owes it to the church.

2) Social scientists need to do more work on the sociology and the psychology of the local religious community— which has not progressed very much since the pioneering work of Joseph Fichter in *Southern Parish* almost 40 years ago. Many younger historians are documenting the past of the neighborhood parish but comparative studies of currently functioning parishes are virtually nonexistent. Yet the parish is almost a perfect laboratory for social research and the comparative study of many parishes is a made to order opportunity to test theories of organizational structure. Recent work in New Jersey by Father James Mahoney illustrates how comparative studies of many parishes can be a gold mine both for sociological theory and practical church action.

3) Funding agencies, either diocesan or extra-diocesan, must understand that neither the theological nor the sociological work mentioned in the last two paragraphs can occur unless they are funded, and indeed should not occur unless the funding is adequate so that they can be done properly. Much of what passes as parish social research in this country is embarassingly amateurish and would much better be left undone. The church has survived very well in the United States until the present time without either reflecting on or evaluating scientifically what it does in the local religious community. Our point in this book, however, is that we have now come to a time when a combination of factors, not least of which is a confusion on the part of the parish clergy as to what comes next, makes it

essential that we begin to both reflect and analyze. A continuation of the old policy of blundering ahead unreflectively with band-aid responses and ad hoc solutions will no longer work.

To Seminary Faculties and
Clergy Education Personnel

1) We reject any "practical" training experiences which interfere with the intellectual and imaginative development of the clergy, present or future. Skills of mind and imagination are finally the most practical tools of the ministry. The training of a person's powers of thought and expression ought not be squeezed to the margins of clerical education by a misguided emphasis on "pastoral" experience.

2) Such "pastoral" experiences, which are integrated into the intellectual and imaginative development of the priest, ought to be heavily oriented towards "apprenticeship," that is, work with those who are master craftpersons at the necessary skills. A "deacon" year or a "pastoral" year ought not to be merely hanging around a parish but an experience rigorously shaped in the direction of acquiring certain ministerial skills—preaching, listening, comforting, challenging; and there should be sufficient feedback in these interludes so that the future priest can be confident that he is growing in skills.

3) The continuing education of the clergy ought to involve considerable amounts of reflection on the meaning of pastoral experience. While such things as Scripture Institutes are admirable, there also should be institutes in which priests are given the opportunity to reflect on their min-

istry with the resources of scripture and theology (and even the social sciences) present to assist such reflection.

4) There is no more important task for continuing education of the clergy than the improvement of the quality of Sunday preaching, an improvement which necessarily means the enhancement of the clerical imagination.

To Bishops

None of the recommendations made previously will stand much likelihood of being successful unless you take the lead in promoting them. In the local religious community we call the neighborhood parish you have one of the most remarkable institutions for the ministry of the church which has ever been developed. In your parish clergy you have some of the most outstanding religious leaders the world has ever known. However, the changes which have occurred in Catholicism in this country in the last four decades have created a crisis in the parish ministry which will not be resolved unless there is confident and visionary leadership from bishops. You must be convinced of the worth of the local religious leader, even if sometimes he is not. You must see the big picture which transcends all the little pictures in your diocese BUT WHICH INCLUDES ALL OF THEM. You must believe, not only verbally, but in your gut that the church exists at its most special and most intense, not in the chancery office, not in the roman curia, but on a Sunday morning when a parish priest is preaching to his congregation or on a Sunday evening when a husband and wife are driving home silently in their car, thinking about the problems they will face in the week ahead. Whatever you do that facilitates those two ministerial situations par excellence is work worthy of a bishop. Whatever does not facilitate them might merit reexamination.

To the Lay People

Finally, gentle souls, you pay the bill; and finally you get what you deserve in the way of religious leadership. If you want the kind of priests we have described in this book, ultimately you'll get them, though you may have to insist very loudly indeed. And if you don't get them, in the last analysis you will have only yourself to blame.

Notes

Chapter 1

1. By myth we mean a symbolic story which demonstrates, as Alan Watts says, "the inner meaning of the universe end of human life". The stories about Mary, Seat of Wisdom, are the stories of how the people of the community find their parish giving meaning to their lives. They are not fantasies; rather they are ways of representing to themselves and to those beyond the parish the deep truths they find available in their community life.

2. The theme of the Wisdom Weekends has been the challenge to us today to continue Jesus' work of proclaiming the Kingdom of God. The various presentations revolve around how everyone has experienced the challenge in their everyday lives. This theme is often referred to by people when they are trying to explain what makes the parish work for them or when they would like to encourage others to participate in activities inside the parish and also the community. Certainly for about 300 or more people in the parish, this seems to be the common faith.

Chapter 3

1. For a more detailed analysis, see: Andrew M. Greeley, "Sociology and Theology: Some Methodological Questions", *Proceedings of the Thirty-Second Annual Convention* (New York: Catholic Theological Society of America, 1977).

2. Limit experiences are those experiences which confront us with the need for some deeper explanation than we have heretofore been able to find. It requires that we go beyond ourselves and, generally, that we eventually need an explanation that transcends all human capacity for rational scientific explanation.

3. A communal Catholic is one who is strongly identified with the Catholic community but is rather uninterested in the organized church. See: Andrew M. Greeley, *The Communal Catholic: A Personal Manifesto* (New York: Seabury Press, 1976).

Chapter 4

1. For more detailed analysis, see: David Tracy, *The Analogical Imagination* (New York: Seabury Press, 1981).

Chapter 5

1. Mary G. Durkin, *The Suburban Woman: Her Changing Role in the Church* (New York: Seabury Press, 1976).

Chapter 12

1. We have avoided the term professional because of some of the negative connotations associated with it. We find the priesthood (and all religious leadership) in need of something *more* than book knowledge and quickly acquired skills that border on the gimicky. Rather it seems that there is a need for discipline in acquiring skills and at the same time there is a need for the spontaneity of the artist in applying those skills to particular situations. Hence, "disciplined skills and art" goes beyond professionalism.

Chapter 14

1. Hans Kung, *Does God Exist? An Answer for Today* (Garden City, Doubleday & Company, Inc., 1980).

2. Though we are speaking of priest in this instance, the same applies to all religious leaders.

Bibliography

Works by the authors containing assumptions which are the foundations of this project. The reader may consult these works for more detailed background information.

Durkin, Mary G. *The Suburban Woman: Her Changing Role in the Church* (New York: Seabury Press, 1976).

Greeley, Andrew M., *The American Catholic: A Social Portrait* (New York: Basic Books, Inc., 1977).

_____, *The Communal Catholic: A Personal Manifesto* (New York: Seabury Press, 1976).

_____, ed. *The Family in Crisis or in Transition* (New York: Seabury Press, 1979) includes articles by the five authors.

_____, "Sociology and Theology: Some Methodological Questions", *Proceedings of the Thirty-Second Annual Convention* (New York: The Catholic Theological Society of America, 1977).

McCready, William C., "The Generation Gap and the Future of the Church", *Concilium: International Review of Theology,* June, 1975.

_____, "The Irish Neighborhood: A Contribution to American Urban Life", *America and Ireland, 1776–1976,* ed. David Doyle (Westport, CT: Greenwood Press, 1980).

_____, "Pastoral Agenda for the American Church: Non-Practicing Catholics", *The New Catholic World,* January, 1979.

_____, "Social Utilities in a Pluralistic Society", *The Diverse Society: Implications for Social Policy,* ed. Leon Chestang and Pastora Cafferty. National Association of Social Workers, Washington, DC, 1976.

_____, *The Ultimate Values of the American Population* (Beverly Hills: Sage Library of Social Research, No. 23, 1976).

Shea, John, *Stories of Faith* (Chicago: Thomas More Press, 1980).

_____, *Stories of God: An Unauthorized Biography* (Chicago: Thomas More Press, 1978).

Tracy, David, *The Analogical Imagination* (New York: Seabury Press, 1981).

_____, *Blessed Rage for Order* (New York: Seabury Press, 1975).

_____, "The Catholic Analogical Imagination", *Proceedings of the Thirty-Second Annual Convention* (New York: The Catholic Theological Society of America, 1977).